THE
ROAD-BOOKS & ITINERARIES
OF GREAT BRITAIN
1570 to 1850

CAMBRIDGE
UNIVERSITY PRESS

University Printing House, Cambridge CB2 8BS, United Kingdom

Cambridge University Press is part of the University of Cambridge.

It furthers the University's mission by disseminating knowledge in the pursuit of education, learning and research at the highest international levels of excellence.

www.cambridge.org
Information on this title: www.cambridge.org/9781107452794

© Cambridge University Press 1924

First published 1924
First paperback edition 2014

A catalogue record for this publication is available from the British Library

ISBN 978-1-107-45279-4 Paperback

¶The high wayes from any nota-
ble towne in England to the Citie of London. And lykewise from one notable
towne to an other, newly collected
and set forth in a more larger &
better maner then hereto-
fore it hath ben.

¶From S. Buryen in Cornewal to Exceſter.

From S. Buryen to the Mount   xx. mile
from the Mount to Truro   xij. mile
from Truro to Bodmin   xij. mile
from Bodmin to Launston   xx. mile
from Launston to Okhampton   xb. mile
from Okhampton to Crockhorneswel   x. mile
from Crockhorneswel to Exceſter   x. mile
            From Exceter to London.
¶From Exceſter to Honiton   xij. mile
from Honiton to Charde   x. mile
from Charde to Crokehorne   bi. mile
from Crokehorne to Sherborne   x. mile
from Sherborne to Shaftesbury   xij. mile
from Shaftesbury to Salſbury   xbiij. m
from Saliſbury to Andouer   xb. mi
from Andouer to Baſingſtoke   xbi. mile
from Baſingſtoke to Hertlerow   biij. m
from Hertlerow to Bagſhot   biij. mi
from Bagſhot to Stanes   biij. mi
from Stanes to London   xb. mile
¶There is an other way from Exceter to London, and in manner as neere, whiche ſome do ac-
compt the better way, that is.
from Exceſter to Honyton   xij. mile
from Honiton to Burport   xbi. mile
from Burport to Dorcheſter   xij. mile
from Dorcheſter to Blandforde   xij. mile
from Blandford to Saliſbury   xx. mile   and
                Ii. iiij.

A PAGE FROM TABLES OF HIGHWAYS
in *Graftons Abridgement of the Chronicles of Englande*,
edition of 1572

THE
ROAD-BOOKS & ITINERARIES
OF GREAT BRITAIN
1570 TO 1850

A CATALOGUE

WITH AN INTRODUCTION AND
A BIBLIOGRAPHY

BY

SIR HERBERT GEORGE FORDHAM

Author of *Hertfordshire Maps: a Descriptive Catalogue
of the Maps of the County, 1579–1900; The Cartography
of the Provinces of France, 1570–1757; Studies in
Carto-Bibliography; Catalogue des Guides-Routiers et des
Itinéraires Français, 1552–1850; Maps, their History,
Characteristics and Uses; The Road-Books and Itineraries
of Ireland, 1647–1850,* and other works

CAMBRIDGE
AT THE UNIVERSITY PRESS
1924

INTRODUCTION

IN offering to the public, and to bibliographers in particular, a revised and amplified catalogue of the Road-Books and Itineraries of Great Britain it will probably be convenient if I incorporate in this Introduction some sections of the introductory paper with which the original catalogue published in 1916 was associated*.

The first point with which I then dealt was, naturally, one of definition.

It is, evidently, difficult to establish an exclusive and rigid classification of Road-Books.

On the one hand are found descriptions of journeys which have a systematic character, and so far describe the road followed as to be in the nature of an itinerary, and, on the other, maps in which roads are a predominant feature. Neither of these prints can, however, be properly classed as road-books.

My definition excludes all topographical matter in which road-distances, with the stages of ordinary travel, are not incorporated as a distinctive feature; as regards maps, I include those only of which the object is to set out individual roads, and which are, in general, grouped together as a book, or atlas, prepared for the use of travellers. The actual record, in the form of a description, of the route to be followed by a traveller on a road, or series of roads, with the stages of ordinary travel set out, is essential in the classification of road-books and itineraries bibliographically.

Such works vary from a mere enumeration of stages on a road, with the distances between them, to an elaborate and full descriptive text, giving, from mile to mile, both the character of the roadway itself, and details of the adjacent country on either side of that roadway and of all the objects of present, or historical, interest accessible, or seen from the line of route.

* Road-Books and Itineraries Bibliographically considered. Transactions of the Bibliographical Society, Vol. XIII. London, 1916. 4°.

Similarly, road-maps also vary from a barely outlined highway, with distances and some slight particulars, to the delineation of wide strips of country on either side of the road dealt with, showing the character of the districts through which it passes in great detail.

The modern guide-book may be pretty generally excluded from this bibliographical grouping, as being a work in which the indications of route are entirely subordinate to its general descriptive objects; but, it must be admitted that, in such a classification, it is difficult to find an absolute and clear line of distinction which separates guide-books from itineraries, and the tendency latterly has certainly been, in consequence, no doubt, of the great increase of motor-traffic and of pleasure tours by road, towards giving a road-book form to publications issued for the guidance of tourists.

Ordinary topographical works sometimes approach the itinerary in character, or contain statements of road-distances and modes of travel separately dealt with in the text. Some of such publications must thus be regarded, as to these special features, as road-books.

Modern railway time-tables may be safely omitted, as publications standing altogether apart, though here again some road-book features exist, and, in the quite early days of railway travel, descriptions of the railroads in the road-book form were published, of which, perhaps, the earliest is the "Appendix to Mogg's Pocket Itinerary; being a Description of the Rail Roads," which appeared in 1837.

The number of original titles in the Catalogue which follows does not, as may easily be imagined, represent the productivity of the British press in this matter. Comparatively few road-books and itineraries exist as a single issue, or edition, and many of them have been reprinted over long periods, with continual improvements in the text and maps and with additions to their size and to the information they offer to the traveller. A few examples of their periodical publication may be cited.

The *Britannia Depicta*, founded on John Ogilby's *Britannia* of 1675 and 1698, first appeared in 1720, and continued to be printed in successive issues until 1764. The complete series does not seem to be yet established.

Based on the same materials, is an epitome of the text of Ogilby, which had an even longer range, namely from 1676 to 1794, with a title varied from time to time, but generally known as "The Traveller's Pocket-Book." The "*Vade Mecum*, or the Necessary Companion," published originally by John Playford, and which incorporated tables of roads, had a range from at least 1679 to 1772, though very few issues can be identified, and "Owen's New Book of Roads" is a road-book of a later period which had a long career. I have not found the first edition of this publication. The second is of 1779, and others are known of 1784, 1788, 1796, 1802, 1805, 1808, 1814, 1822, 1827 and 1840. Paterson's well-known itinerary ("A New & Accurate Description of all the Direct & Principal Cross Roads in Great Britain") began its existence in 1771, as a thin, octavo volume of but xxiv + 77 pages of text; it continued to be published at irregular intervals, until, in the hands of Edward Mogg, it had attained (in 1829 and some subsequent years) to the dimensions of a large and closely-printed volume of 858 pages, with 13 maps. "Cary's New Itinerary," which appeared in 1798, passed through eleven editions, 1798 (two issues), 1802, 1806, 1812, 1815, 1817, 1819, 1821, 1826 and 1828, and his "Traveller's Companion," of the same period, appeared in a long series, 1790–1828, with thirteen issues. As will be seen also, on referring to the catalogue, some local guides, such, for instance, as those published for Bath and for Tunbridge Wells, had a very long series of editions, now difficult to establish with any completeness.

These are, perhaps, the most striking instance of longevity in British publications of this description, but in France the series of official postal guides had a greater extension, the first issue being of 1708, and their annual, or biennial, publication extending from that year to as late as 1859, under the successive titles of: *Liste Générale des Postes de France, État Général des Postes de France*, etc.

Thus, a catalogue of road-books and itineraries, while it may contain but a comparatively limited number of original titles, must be largely extended by long series of editions under such titles, and these editions must be distinguished by reference in many cases to the growth of the works themselves under various hands, developments which not infrequently constitute them new and original books.

There is some difficulty in assigning a place in connection with this subject to maps and atlases which, while giving roads as a prominent and special feature, and being published with a suitable title, are also of a general character.

Of such works "Cary's Traveller's Companion, or, a Delineation of the Turnpike Roads of England and Wales," already referred to, is a critical example. It is a small, octavo volume of maps of the English counties, with a general map of England and Wales and maps of North Wales and South Wales, 43 in all, with the roads specially delineated and coloured, and with miles marked upon them, and instructions for the use of the maps as guides in travelling. From the third edition (1806) of "Cary's New Itinerary," it is issued of even date with that work, and is often found bound up with it. Such an atlas, and others of a similar character, can hardly be omitted from a catalogue of road-books, but it is difficult, obviously, to draw a line between these and other cartographical publications in which roads are a special though not a predominant feature.

Other publications which come near enough to itineraries to be grouped with them, as having a common object, are the various tables of distances, which, in book form, owe their origin to John Norden, who, in 1625, published his "Intended Guyde, For English Travailers," a set of such tables for England and Wales and each of the English counties separately. This was followed by a succession of reductions, published under the titles: "A Direction for the English Traviller" (1635, 1636, 1643, 1677 and 1680), and "A Book of the Names of all Parishes, Market Towns ＊ ＊ ＊ in England and Wales" (1657, 1662, 1668 and 1677). Norden's tables were copied in the *Magna Britannia et Hibernia* of 1720, and, as to the form and arrangement, have been utilised in a whole series of publications, both here and abroad, down to the present time.

Another book of the same sort, which may be taken as typical, is Paterson's "A Travelling Dictionary: or, Alphabetical Tables ✳ ✳ ✳ being a second part to the New & Accurate Description of the Roads," which, though issued separately, is commonly found bound up at the end of the "Description." The "Dictionary" ran through eight editions (1772 to 1799).

It is with these inclusions that I make up a catalogue, as complete and exhaustive as the materials available allow, of the original titles of the Road-books and Itineraries of Great Britain, setting out, in addition, all the numerous reprints, re-issues and editions which are known to exist.

The original catalogue, as printed in 1916, was a fairly complete work, including everything noted up to the date of publication, and subsequent research has, as regards the eighteenth and nineteenth centuries, produced very little additional matter of interest, and nothing of any real importance.

The additions and insertions made for this period in the catalogue as now published, and for Great Britain alone, are mainly of titles of local guides and itineraries connected with the development of fashionable bathing and sea-side centres, and of those of editions previously unknown of road-books already catalogued.

Guides to centres of health and amusement in which tables of roads of access are incorporated, are, in the century commencing about 1750, numerous altogether out of proportion to their intrinsic interest, but their inclusion in any catalogue of itineraries seems necessary for its bibliographical completeness, and they are, therefore, added, to the number of between forty and fifty.

They first appear about 1750, the date attributed, doubtfully, to the earliest known issue (the second) of "The Tradesman's & Traveller's Pocket Companion: or, The Bath and Bristol Guide," published at Bath, and this is followed, a few years later (about 1762), by "The New Bath Guide," which ran through a number of editions, under slightly varied titles, up to as late as 1853.

Bath and Bristol, as fashionable resorts, seem to have had little vogue, however, beyond the end of the eighteenth century; Tunbridge Wells,

Brighton and Weymouth, Cheltenham and Buxton all came into road-book literature in the period 1780–1790.

The guides to Tunbridge Wells and Brighton, distinguished by details of the roads of approach, continued to be published until 1851 and 1824 respectively.

Weymouth appears to have had only a dozen, or so, years of special popularity, but Cheltenham guides, with itineraries, range from 1783 to 1841.

Hastings and Scarborough became popular just at the end of the eighteenth century, and a Buxton guide was published, in successive editions, 1790 to 1818.

Tours in special areas—the Lake District, Wales, and the Highlands of Scotland—first appear amongst road-books in 1778, 1795 and 1798, respectively, and itineraries of these districts for the use of tourists are thereafter numerous.

Thus it may be said that travelling for pleasure and in search of health had its earliest development on systematic lines in Great Britain in the middle of the eighteenth century, and was concentrated on certain centres, of which Bath, Bristol, Tunbridge Wells, Brighton and Cheltenham were the most important, and that tourism, as known in modern times, had its rise in journeys through the mountainous areas of England, Wales and Scotland towards the end only of that century.

In the earlier period, that of the publication of the first tables of the highways in the sixteenth and seventeenth centuries, a larger field of view has been opened up by the appearance of Bosanquet's important study of the early English almanacks*, which shows that in this class of publications, and in others allied with them, tables of the English highways were incorporated from at least as early as 1571 (Richard Grafton's "A litle treatise").

Following up this clue through the next century, we find a large number of almanacks and prognostications which contain short lists of

---

* "English Printed Almanacks & Prognostications. A Bibliographical History to the year 1600." By Eustace F. Bosanquet. London, 1917. 4°.

the roads of England and Wales, and this practice of printing road-tables in almanacks persists up to and beyond the middle of the eighteenth century, and, in some cases, extends even into the early part of the nineteenth.

In the catalogue, as now printed, while all the almanacks containing tables of roads which are recorded by Bosanquet are inserted, no attempt has been made to establish an exhaustive list of later almanacks and their annual issues, involving, as it would, very tedious and uninteresting bibliographical research, without, as regards the present subject, any adequate results. The examples catalogued later than 1600 are sufficient to show the development of road-book literature in connection with almanacks in the period dealt with, and have been selected as representative specimens with that object.

In France the printing of tables of highways in almanacks and other ephemeral publications seems never to have been customary. It was specially forbidden in the licence accorded to Alexis Hubert Jaillot, in 1708, for the printing of the semi-official *Liste Générale des Postes de France*, and the publication of such tables in the *Almanach Royal*, which had made a beginning in the previous year, only continued until 1710*.

In addition to what appeared in almanacks in the sixteenth century in England, similar, and in some cases identical tables of roads are found in Richard Grafton's "Abridgement of the Chronicles of Englande," from 1570, and in the later editions of John Stow's "Summarie of the Chronicles of England," a rival publication, from 1575.

Thus, the early period of publication of regular itineraries of the roads of England and Wales is considerably reinforced with examples of an uniform type which had escaped notice up to the time of printing the catalogue of 1916, and it may now be said that, for a full century before the appearance of John Ogilby's *Britannia*, in 1675, tables of the principal British highways, in a handy form, based on the old British miles

---

* See "The *Listes Générales des Postes de France*, 1708–79, and the Jaillots, *géographes ordinaires du Roi*." Transactions of the Bibliographical Society—The Library. London, 1922. 4°.

of 1500 Roman paces, or 2220 metres, equivalent to 2428 statute yards*, were continuously available for the use of travellers. These tables were uniformly associated with lists of fairs, necessary as information for commercial purposes, the principal objects of the traveller in those times. The tables of money and of exchange published on the continent of Europe from quite the beginning of the sixteenth century, have, it may be noted, no counterpart in the British Isles, where diversity of coinage and of standards of value, was of small importance, as compared with the difficulty arising in central Europe from the great variety introduced by both national currencies and the numerous special coinages of the cities of Germany†.

The tables of highways published in Great Britain in the latter part of the sixteenth and the first half of the seventeenth centuries have a certain parallelism with the early French road-books, *La Guide des Chemins de France*, and *Les Voyages de plusieurs endroits de France; et encores de la Terre Saincte, d'Espaigne, d'Italie, et autres pays*, of Charles Estienne, of which the editions now known are of the following years and places:—1552 (1st edition), 1552 (2nd edition), 1553, all of Paris; 1553, Rouen; 1554, 1555, 1560, Paris; 1566, Lyons; 1570 (*c.*), Paris; 1580, Lyons; 1583, Paris; 1583 (*Suite*), Lyons; 1586, 1588, 1599, Paris; 1600, Rouen; 1610 (*Suite*), Lyons, and 1612 and 1623, Troyes, and the *Sommaire Description de la France, Allemagne, Italie et Espagne, avec la guide des chemins pour aller et venir par les provinces, et aux villes*

---

* See "Customary Acres & their Historical Importance," Part II, "The Old British Mile." By Frederic Seebohm. London, 1914. 8°.

† A good example of this diversity is furnished by the *Petit Traicté des Métaux et Monnoyes fort utile pour le Voyager*, printed at the end of the *Sommaire Description de la France, Allemagne, Italie et Espagne*, of Théodore de Mayerne-Turquet, first published at Geneva in 1591. Mayerne-Turquet gives tables of twenty different currencies for Germany alone. The same subject is elaborately dealt with, more than a century and a half later, by the Abbé Expilly, in his *Géographe Manuel* (Paris, 1757–1803), in which, besides tables of the routes from Paris to the principal town of France, and to the principal towns of the world, are to be found two long series of tables headed, respectively: *Des Monnoies et des Changes, Des principales Places de l'Europe, en correspondance avec Paris*, and *Table de Réductions de presque toutes les Espèces de l'Europe au pied courant des Espèces de France, suivant l'ordre Alphabétique*.

plus renommées de ces quatre regions de Théodore de Mayerne-Turquet, of which the recorded issues are:—1591 and 1592, Geneva; 1596, Lyons; 1604, 1606 and 1615, Rouen; 1618, Geneva; 1624, 1629, 1640 and 1642, Rouen, and, finally, 1653, Geneva*.

These, however, are much more complete specimens of systematic itineraries, and have a more distinct bibliographical character than anything published in the British Isles prior to the date of Ogilby's *Britannia*.

I have not yet succeeded in tracing the German publication from which Richard Rowlands translated his "Post of the World" (1576). He, no doubt, drew also upon Estienne, and upon the Italian itinerary he mentions, which was, probably, one published in Lyons in 1572, of which a copy exists in the Baudrier collection, now in the Château de Terrebasse (Isère), France†.

In such enquiries as I have been able to make into the matter, I have not carried back German road-book literature to an earlier date than 1597. A publication of this year‡ contains 187 roads on the continent of Europe, besides eleven highways from London to various parts of England and Wales. It is possible that an earlier edition of this itinerary may have been the foundation of Rowlands' book of 1576. In a later German publication (*Das geöfnete Teutschland,* by Benjamin Schillern, Hamburg, 1700. 12°), which gives a list of "*Scribenten,*" no itineraries are recorded of an earlier date than 1614, although the series of German topographical works of the road-book type there given seems pretty complete for the seventeenth century. In the *Bibliotheca Geographica*

---

* See *Catalogue des Guides-Routiers et des Itinéraires Français, 1552–1850. Bulletin de la Section de Géographie, 1919.* Paris (*Imprimerie nationale*), 1920. 8°. *Illustrations Supplémentaires.* Cambridge, 1921. 8°. And see also "The Earliest French Itineraries, 1552 and 1591. Charles Estienne and Théodore de Mayerne-Turquet." Transactions of the Bibliographical Society—The Library. London, 1921. 4°.

† *Poste per diverse parti del mondo & Il viaggio di S. Jacomo di Galitia. Con tutte le Fieri notabili, che si fanno per tutto il mondo. Con una breve narratione delle sette Chiese di Roma. Aggiuntoni di nuoue, il viaggio di Gierusalem, Con alcune altre poste mai piu poste in luce.* (Lyons, Benoist Rigaud, 1572. 16°.) In the address to the reader this book is stated to have been written by Cherubinus de Stella.

‡ *Kronn und Auszbundt aller Wegweiser,* including: *Wegzaiger ausz etlichen vornehmen Stätten von Englandt.*

Germaniae of Paul Emil Richter (Leipsic, 1896), nothing in the nature of a road-book anterior to 1577 occurs, except, possibly, one or two of doubtful date.

Nevertheless, there is a field in Germany for further investigation, and an important foundation may be found in the road-map of that and the adjoining countries of as early a date as 1501 recently republished in Berlin in facsimile, with a memoir by the late Dr Wolkenhauer*, one of the victims of the great war.

Apart from the results of this more extended review of the early development of the road-book literature in central Europe during the latter half of the sixteenth century, which has importance in connection with the growth of the same species of literature in England at that period, there is nothing of consequence to add to what I have already said here and elsewhere, but I may draw attention to the short bibliography at the end of this Introduction, grouping the titles of what I have been able to publish, up to the present time, bearing on Road-Books, Itineraries and systematic travel in the British Islands and central Europe, and to which reference may be made on the general subject of road-books and itineraries and their character and bibliographical classification.

The removal of the road-books of Ireland from their incorporation in the general list as printed in 1916 for the whole of the British Islands, is justified both by convenience and by the fact that no such geographical continuity exists between the roads of England and Ireland as is naturally found between those of the different parts of Great Britain itself. The road-books of Ireland are now separately catalogued, and this catalogue, published by the Bibliographical Society of Ireland, at Dublin, may be consulted in the Transactions of that Society.

This second edition of the British Catalogue should be regarded as the definitive one, for it seems improbable that anything additional of more than trifling consequence in the class of literature it deals with can now remain undiscovered.

---

* *Erhard Etzlaubs Reisekarte durch Deutschland*, 1501. *Mit einem Begleittext von Prof. Dr W. Wolkenhauer*. Berlin, 1919. Fol.

It contains 246 original titles, of which 24 are of foreign road-books of, or including, British roads, and principally published abroad. The reprints, re-issues and new editions are very numerous, and, as has been already noticed, in many cases range over a long period of time.

Of the numbers given above the exclusively Scottish road-books are only 24, ranging from 1681 to 1840, including those published abroad. Of Welsh road-books there appear to be only about 20, though it will be observed that the postal routes from London to the principal sea-port towns of Wales are set out from the sixteenth century in the general tables of highways, in connection, no doubt, with the through communication between the metropolis and Ireland.

The issue of this revised and enlarged catalogue as an independent volume obviates the inconvenience of searching for a record of this character in the publications of a Society, however well known that Society may be.

I trust that this re-impression may thus become of acknowledged utility, and it is with this hope that I commend it to bibliographers, historians and my fellow students.

H. G. F.

ODSEY,
  December 1st, 1923.

BIBLIOGRAPHY

An Itinerary of the Sixteenth Century. *La Guide des Chemins d'Angleterre*. Jean Bernard, Paris, 1579. *Cambridge*, 1910. 8°.

Notes on British and Irish Itineraries and Road-Books. *Hertford*, 1912. 8°.

Studies in Carto-Bibliography, British and French, and in the bibliography of Itineraries and Road-Books. *Oxford*, Clarendon Press, 1914. 8°.

Roads and Travel before Railways in Hertfordshire and elsewhere. (Transactions of the Hertfordshire Natural History Society.) *Hertford*, 1915. 8°.

Road-Books and Itineraries bibliographically considered. [With a Catalogue of the Road-Books and Itineraries of Great Britain and Ireland to the year 1850.] (Transactions of the Bibliographical Society.) *London*, 1916. 4°.

Catalogue des Guides-Routiers et des Itinéraires Français, 1552–1850. (*Bulletin de la Section de Géographie*, 1919.) *Paris, Imprimerie nationale*, 1920. 8°.

Catalogue des Guides-Routiers et des Itinéraires Français, 1552–1850. *Illustrations Supplémentaires*. *Cambridge*, 1921. 8°.

The Earliest French Itineraries, 1552 and 1591. Charles Estienne and Théodore de Mayerne-Turquet. (Transactions of the Bibliographical Society—The Library.) *London*, Oxford University Press, 1921. 4°.

Une Piraterie Littéraire au dix-septième siècle. Les contrefaçons de la Liste Générale des Postes de France des Jaillot, 1708–1779. *Cambridge*, University Press, 1922. 8°.

The *Listes Générales des Postes de France*, 1708–1779 and the Jaillots, *géographes ordinaires du Roi*. (Transactions of the Bibliographical Society—The Library.) *London*, Oxford University Press, 1922. 4°.

The Road-Books & Itineraries of Ireland, 1647 to 1850. A Catalogue. (Transactions of the Bibliographical Society of Ireland.) *Dublin*, 1923. 8°.

A CATALOGUE OF THE ROAD-BOOKS
AND ITINERARIES OF GREAT BRITAIN
1570 TO 1850

[*Leland, John.* The Itinerary of John Leland, in or about the years 1535–43.]

(See below, 1710–12.)

Grafton, Richard. Graftons Abridgement of the Chronicles of Englande. Newly & diligently corrected, & finished the last of October, 1570. London, 1570. 12°.

Tables of roads are bound in at the end of the copy in the British Museum, but are imperfect and are not paged or mentioned in the table of contents of the volume. The earlier editions, of 1562, 1563 and 1564, have no roads.

—— Graftons Abridgement of the Chronicles of Englande, newly corrected & augmented, to thys present yere of our Lord. 1572. And in thende of thys Abridgement is added a propre & necessary Treatise, conteynyng many good Rules, & specially one excellent maner of Computacion of yeres, wherby you maye readely finde the date & yeres of any euidēce. The particuler contentes of this Booke appereth in the next page folowing. London, 1572. 12°.

At the end: "Londini, In aedibus Richardi Tottell. Cum Priuilegio. 1572." The last two paragraphs of "The Contentes of this booke" are: "All the Principal Faires in a more orderlye maner then hath ben heretofore set forthe. The high wayes also from one towne to an other muche larger then before hath ben set forthe." The fairs are headed: "The Moneth, day & place, of all the principall Faires kept in England, more orderly & largelier set forth then heretofore hath ben." They make up eight pages, followed by the highways in ten. The latter, headed as in Grafton's "A litle treatise," of 1571 and 1572, are set exactly as in the edition of that publication of 1572, that is to say in ten pages, in lieu of the nineteen pages of the earlier issue, and are followed by the same imprint.

Grafton, Richard. A litle treatise, conteyning many proper Tables & rules, very necessary for the vse of al men, The contentes whereof appere in the next page folowing, Collected & set forthe by Richardi Grafton. London, 1571. 12°.

The contents include "All the Principall Faires* in a more orderlye maner then hath ben heretofore set forthe. The high wayes also from one towne to an other moche larger then before hath ben set forth." The roads fill nineteen pages, arranged in single column, and are headed: "The high wayes from any notable towne in England to the Citie of London. And lykewise from one notable towne to an other, newly collected & set forth in a more larger & better maner then heretofore it hath ben." They are divisible into fifteen main routes to London, with twenty-three branch and cross-roads and alternative routes. The former are: (i) Saint Burien to Exeter and London; (ii) Helford to Southampton and London; (iii) Bristol to London; (iv) Berwick to York and London; (v) Saint David's to London; (vi) Carmarthen to London; (vii) Carnarvon to Chester and London; (viii) Cockermouth to Lancaster and Coventry, and so to London; (ix) Cambridge to London; (x) Oxford to London; (xi) Dover to London; (xii) Rye to London; (xiii) Yarmouth to Colchester and London; (xiv) Walsingham to London, and (xv) Yarmouth to Norwich and London.

— *Another issue.* London, 1572. 12°.

The roads are re-set in ten pages.

— A brief treatise conteinyng many proper Tables & easie rules, verie necessary & needeful, for the vse & commoditie of all people, collected out of certaine learned mens workes. The contentes whereof, the Page that followeth doeth expresse. Newly set fourth & allowed, accordyng to the Queenes Maiesties Iniunctions, Imprinted at London by Ihon Waley. London, [*c.* 1573?]. 12°.

— *Another issue.* London, 1576. 12°.

— *Another issue.* London, 1579. 12°.

— *Another issue.* London, 1582. 12°.

W. W. Another issue, "perused, corrected, & augmented by W. W." London, 1591. 12°.

— *Another issue.* London, 1593. 12°.

— *Another issue.* London, 1595. 12°.

— *Another issue.* London, 1596. 12°.

— *Another issue.* London, 1611. 12°.

* Tables of fairs are first found in 1556, in Digges' "Prognostication Everlasting." They first occur in an almanack in 1560, in Henry Rocheforth's "An Almanack & prognosticatiō for this yere of our Lorde God M.DLX."

More, Philip. An Almanack & Prognostication for xxxvii yeres, very profitable for all men, specially for Phisitions Chirurgions, men of Law, Marchants, Mariners husbandmen, & handicraftes men: ✳ ✳ ✳ Gathered by Philip More, practicioner in Phisicke & Chirurgerie. Imprinted at London by Henrie Binneman & Henrie Saunderson, & are to be solde in the Bursse at the 3. crownes Imperiall. London, 1571. 12°.

— *Another issue.* London, 1573. 12°.

Stow, John. A Summarie of the Chronicles of England, from the first coming of Brute into this land, vnto this present yeare of Christ 1575. Diligently collected, corrected & enlarged, by John Stowe Citizen of London. Imprinted at London by Richard Tottle & Henry Binneman. Cum priuilegio. London, 1575. 12°.

Contains, in addition to a list of fairs, tables of roads headed: "How a man may iourney from any notable towne in Englande, to the Citye of London, or from London to any notable towne in the Realme," giving the following nine roads: (i) Walsingham to London; (ii) Berwick to York and London; (iii) Carnarvon to Chester and London; (iv) Cockermouth to Lancaster and London; (v) Yarmouth to Colchester and London; (vi) Dover to London; (vii) Saint Burien to London; (viii) Bristol to London, and (ix) Saint David's to London. This is the earliest edition in which the highways appear.

— *Another edition.* London, 1579. 12°.

— *Another edition.* London, 1584. 12°.

— *Another edition.* London, 1587. 12°.

— *Another edition.* London, 1590. 12°.

— *Another edition.* London, 1598. 12°.

— *Another edition.* London, 1604. 12°.

H., E. The Abridgement of the English Chronicle, First collected by M. John Stow, & after him augmented with very many memorable Antiquities, & continued with matters foreine & domesticall, vnto the beginning of the yeare, 1618. By E. H. Gentleman. London, 1618. Sm. 8°.

To the table of roads is added a route from Carlisle to Doncaster and London.

Rowlands, Richard. The Post of the World. Wherein is contayned the antiquities & originall of the most famous Cities in Europe. With their trade & traficke. With their wayes & distance of myles, from country to country. With the true & perfect knowledge of their Coynes, the places of their Mynts: with al their Martes & Fayres. And the Raignes of all the Kinges of England. A booke right necessary & profitable, for all sortes of persons, the like before this tyme not Imprinted. London, 1576. 12°.

A second title runs: "The Post for divers partes of the world: to travaile from one notable Citie unto an other, with a descripcion of the antiquities of divers famous Cities of Europe. The contents doe further apeare in the next leafe folowing. Very necessary & profitable for Gentlemen, Marchants, Factors, or any other persons disposed to travaile. The like not heretofore in English."

The roads in England are: (i) Dover to London; (ii) Oxford to London; (iii) Bristol to London; (iv) York to London; (v) Berwick to York, and (vi) Saint David's to London.

Holinshed, Raphael. The Chronicles of England, Scotlande, & Irelande, conteyning the description & Chronicles of England, from the first inhabiting unto the conquest. The description & Chronicles of Scotland, from the first originall of the Scottes nation, till the yeare of our Lorde. 1571. The description & Chronicles of Yrelande, likewise from the firste originall of that Nation untill the yeare 1547. Faithfully gathered & set forth, by Raphaell Holinshed. 3 vol. London, 1577. Fol.

Contains, besides "The principall Faires Kept in Englande," the highways of England, under the heading: "How a man may journey from any notable towne in England, to the Citie of London, or from London to any notable towne in the Realme," with the roads as follows· (i) Walsingham to London; (ii) Berwick to York and London; (iii) Carnarvon to Chester and London; (iv) Cockermouth to Lancaster and London; (v) Yarmouth to Colchester and London; (vi) Dover to London; (vii) Saint Burien to London; (viii) Bristol to London; (ix) Saint David's to London; (x) Dover to Cambridge; (xi) Canterbury to Oxford, and (xii) London to Cambridge. This table follows that of Stow (1575 above) with the addition of the roads numbered x to xii. It is followed by a table headed "Of certeine waies in Scotland, out of Regnald Wolfes his Annotations," containing seven routes: (i) Berwick to Edinburgh; (ii) Edinburgh to Berwick (another way); (iii) Edinburgh to Dumbarton; (iv) Stirling to Kinghorn; (v) Kinghorn to the Taymouth; (vi) the Taymouth to Stockford in Ross and so to the Nesse of Harben; (vii) Carlisle to Whitehorn.

— *Another edition.* 3 vol. London, 1587. Fol.

— *Another edition.* 6 vol. London, 1807–8. 4°.

Christendom. Itinerarium Orbis Christiani. Itinerario di tutti i Paesi Christiani. Wegweiser des gantzen Christenthumbs. La Guide des chemins de tous les Pais de la Chrestienté. No place, 1579. Sm. obl. 4°.

Atlas of thirty-seven maps of the countries of Europe, including England and Scotland. No roads are shown in Scotland, however, and in England only those (i) from Dover to Gravesend; (ii) from London to Salisbury, and (iii) from London to Lynn through Cambridge with a branch from Cambridge through Thetford to Norwich and Yarmouth.

Bernard, Jean. La Guide des chemins d'Angleterre, fort necessaire à ceux qui y voyagent, ou qui passent de France par Angleterre en Escosse. Paris, 1579. 8°.

— *Another edition.* Paris, 1587. 8°.

Sets out nine roads in England and Wales, namely: (i) Dover to London; (ii) London to Berwick; (iii) London to Walsingham; (iv) Carnarvon to Chester and London; (v) Cockermouth to Lancaster and London; (vi) Yarmouth to Colchester and London; (vii) Saint Burien to London; (viii) Bristol to London, and (ix) Saint David's to London.

Adams, Frank. Writing Tables with a Kalender for xxiiii. yeres, with other necessary rules, the Contents therof you shall finde in the other side of this Leafe. Made at London, by Franke Adams, Stationer & Bookbinder, dwelling in Thames streete, at the signe of yᵉ black Rauen, nere Londō Bridge, & are there to be sold: or else on the Ryal Exchange, at the signe of the halfe Rose, & halfe Sun next to the north doore, by Thomas Frethren. 1581. London, 1581. 36°.

The contents of this book include: "All yᵉ high wayes frō any towne or citie, in Englād, to the citie of London, & the nūber of yᵉ myles. All the principall Fayres in Englād, & where they are kept." The routes set out are: (i) Berwick to York and London; (ii) Cockermouth to Lancaster and London; (iii) Saint David's to Gloucester and London; (iv) Carmarthen to Worcester and London; (v) Carnarvon to Chester and London; (vi) Saint Burien to Exeter and London; (vii) Bristol to London; (viii) Lincoln to London; (ix) Nottingham to Leicester and London; (x) Boston to London; (xi) Cambridge to London; (xii) Oxford to London; (xiii) Dover to London; (xiv) Rye to London; (xv) Yarmouth to Ipswich and London; (xvi) Walsingham to London, and (xvii) Yarmouth to Norwich and London.

— *Another issue.* London, 1598. 36°.

— *Another issue.* London, 1600?. 36°.

— *Another issue.* London, 1604. 36°.

— *Another issue.* London, 1611. 36°.

[*Smith, William.* The Particular Description of England, 1588.]
(See below, 1879.)

Gray, Walter. An Almanacke & Prognostication, made for the yeere of our Lorde. M.D. LXXXIX. And first after the Leape yeere. Rectified for the altitude & Meridian of Dorchester, serving most aptly for the West partes, & generally for all Englande. By Walter Gray, Gentleman. London, 1589. 12°.

Tables of roads are inserted in this almanack, headed: "A perfect direction of the best & rediest hygh wayes, from any notabe (*sic*) Towne in England, to the citie of London, & from the citie of London, to any notable Towne; & Lykewyse from one notabe (*sic*) Towne to another." The roads are those found in "A litle treatise" 1571 and 1572, but arranged in a different order.

— *Another issue.* London, 1595. 12°.

Germany. Kronn und Auszbundt aller Wegweiser. ✳ ✳ ✳ *Gedruckt zu Cölln. Durch L'ambercum Andree. In Jahr* M.D. XCVII. *Cologne,* 1597. 4°.

Includes *Wegzaiger ausz etlichen vornehmen Stätten von Englandt*, and the following English roads: From London (i) to Saint Burien; (ii) to Bristol; (iii) to Saint David's; (iv) to Carnarvon, by Lichfield; (v) to Cockermouth; (vi) to Berwick; (vii) to Lynn; (viii) to Walsingham; (ix) to Yarmouth, by Norwich; (x) to Yarmouth by Ipswich, and (xi) to Calais, by Dover.

[*Hentznerus, Paulus. Itinerarium* ✳ ✳ ✳ *Angliae,* 1598.]
(See below, 1612.)

England. A Table of the chieffest Cities, & Townes in England, as they ly from London, & the distance of miles, howe a man may travill from London to any of them or from any of them to London. London, [*c.* 1610?]. Single sheet.

This is a nearly square wood-cut, containing a circular arrangement of thirteen roads radiating from London, as follows: to York; to Lincoln; to Cambridge; to Norwich; to Yarmouth; to Dover; to Rye; to Southampton; to Exeter; to Bristol; to Hereford; to Worcester, and to Chester, with the stages shown on each route. It is "London Printed by Walter Dight, at the signe of the Harpe in shoo-lane."

Hopton, Arthur. A Concordancy of Yeares. Containing a new, easie, & most exact Computation of Time, according to the English Account. Also the use of the English & Roman Kalender, with briefe Notes, Rules, & Tables, as well Mathematicall & Legal, as Vulgar, for each private Mans Occasion. London, 1612. 12°.

— *Another issue.* London, 1615. 12°.

— *Another issue.* London, 1616. 12°.

— [*Penkethman, John.*] *Another issue,* enlarged. London, 1635. 12°.

Contains "A Geographicall Description of the Wayes from one notable towne to another"; tables of the correct weights of gold coins, and tables of equivalency, with "A briefe remembrance of the principall Faires in England & Wales."

Hentznerus, Paulus. Itinerarium Germaniae, Galliae; Angliae; Italiae; Scriptum à Paulo Hentznero JC. Norimbergae, Sumtibus Autoris, et typis Abrahami Wagenmanni excusum. cIↃ IↃ cXII. Nuremberg. 1612. 4°.

— *Another edition.* Breslau, 1617. 4°.

— *Another edition.* Nuremberg, 1618. 4°.

— *A new edition.* Nuremberg, 1629. 8°.

— *Another edition.* Leipsic, 1661. 8°.

The roads followed are those from Rye to London, London to Cambridge, Cambridge to Oxford, Oxford to London, and London to Dover.

Rudston, John. An Almanacke & Prognostication, for the Yeare of our Lord God, 1615*. By John Rudston Math. London. Printed for the Companie of Stationers. London, [1615]. 8°.

* A large number of rival series of almanacks, prognostications and similar ephemeral publications appeared year by year throughout the seventeenth and eighteenth centuries, and even continued into the nineteenth century, most of them giving tables of the highways of England and Wales in one form or another. It would be extremely cumbersome to insert in this catalogue the whole of the annual production of this long series. Representative titles have, therefore, been selected, which give a sufficient clue to examples fairly covering the whole period and available for study in the public collections. These will be found under the dates [1615]–1619, Rudston (above); 1638, Rivers; 1656–1802, Riders; 1656–1841, Woodhouse; 1686–1712, City & Countrey Chapman's Almanack, etc.; 1705, Traveller's & Chapman's Daily Instructor.

— A Prognostication, for the yeere of our Lord God, 1619. London, 1619. 8°.

In the above is found: "The Geographical description of waies from one notable Towne to another, over all England, & thereby how to travell from any of them to the Citty of London, set forth after a new order by A. H." Fifteen routes are given. Rudston adopts a tabular arrangement not previously used.

Norden, John. England: An Intended Guyde, For English Travailers. Shewing in generall, how far one Citie, & many Shire-Townes in England, are distant from other. Together, with the Shires in perticular: & the Cheife Townes in every of them. With a generall Table, of the most of the principall Townes in Wales. Invented & Collected, By John Norden. London, 1625. 4°.

English Traveller. A Direction for the English Traviller, by which he Shal be inabled to Coast about all England & Wales. And also to know how farre any Market or noteable Towne in any Shire lyeth one from an other, & Whether the same be East, West, North, or South from yᵉ Shire Towne. As also the distance betweene London & any other Shire or great towne: with the scituation thereof East, West, North, or South from London. By the help also of this worke one may know (in what Parish, Village, or Mansion house soever he be in) What Shires, he is to passe thorough & which way he is to travell, till he come to his Journies End. London, 1635. 8°.

— *Another issue.* London, 1636. 8°.

— *Another issue*, with the maps re-engraved on a larger scale. London, 1643. Sm. 4°.

— *Another issue.* London, 1677*. 16°.

— *Another issue.* London, 1680*. 16°.

Rivers, Peregrine. An Almanack for 1638. Cambridge, 1638. 16°.

In this almanack is "A plain description of the high wayes in England & Wales, now the second time enlarged, in a more perfect manner then heretofore hath been published, with the use of the same by example." The roads are arranged in the tabular form introduced by Rudston.

---

* These issues are noted from entries by J. Garrett in the Term Catalogues 28 May, 1677 and May, 1680.

Coulon, Louis. Le fidèle Conducteur pour le voyage d'Angleterre. Montrant, Exactement les Raretez & choses Remarquables qui se trouuent en chaques Villes, & les distances d'icelles, auec un dénombrement des Batailles qui s'y sont données. Par le Sieur Coulon. A Troyes, Chez Nicolas Oudot, Et se vendent, A Paris, Chez Gervais Clouzier, Marchand Libraire au Palais, sur les degrez de la Ste. Chapelle. M. DC. LIV. *Auec Privilege du Roy.* Troyes, 1654. 8°.

The roads shown are, from London (i) to Dover; (ii) to Berwick and into Scotland; (iii) to Walsingham; (iv) to Chester and to Carnarvon in Wales; (v) to Lancaster and to Cockermouth; (vi) to Yarmouth; (vii) to Saint Burien in Cornwall; (viii) to Bristol, and (ix) to Saint David's in Wales, being the same as those in Jean Bernard's Guide of 1579.

Porter, Thomas. A New Booke of Mapps, Being a ready Guide or Direction for any Stranger, or other, who is to Travel in any part of the Cōmon-wealth of England, Scotland, & Ireland. * * * I. Alphabetical Tables, shewing the Longitude & Latitude of all the Towns named in the said Maps; * * * II. Tables of the High-wayes in England, Wales, & Ireland, Alphabetically methodized; which hath made them very plaine. III. Tables as easie as an Almanack * * * And other usefull Tables. By Thomas Porter. London, 1655. 12°.

"Scotlands Alphabetical Table" is found in this little book, but there are no Scottish Roads, only those of England and Ireland being shown.

Riders, Schardanus. [From 1672, *Cardanus Riders*, and from 1727, *Cardanus Rider*.] Riders: 1656. British Merlin: * * * With many necessary Tables, containing directions for such as use Marts & Fairs; also for Travellers that coast the Common-wealth. London, 1656. 12°. [1656–1841.]

Contains "A true & plain Description of the Highways in England & Wales," setting out thirty-eight roads, filling five pages. This almanack appeared annually up to 1841. Roads are given until at least as late as 1802, but had disappeared in the edition of 1805. They continue in 1656 in the form adopted in 1656 to the year 1751; in 1752 they are set in columns, with the heading: "A Table of the principal direct Roads in England & Wales, & of several other Roads which branch out of the direct Roads, Etc. according to the computed & measured Distances," and a text and arrangement differing from those previously used. This table fills six pages. In 1756 the old form is resumed, in five pages, "according to the Measured Distances," and this continued until 1802.

England and Wales. A Book of the Names of all Parishes, Market Towns, Villages, Hamlets, & smallest Places, in England & Wales. Alphabetically set down, as they be in every Shire. With the Names of the Hundreds in which they are, & how many Towns there are in every Hundred. So that naming any Town or Place in England & Wales, you may presently in the Alphabet find it, & know in what Shire & Hundred it is, & so know the distance from it to the Shire Town, & in the large Table for Shires in England how far to London, or from it to any other Town in England. A Work very necessary for Travellers, Quarter-masters, Gatherers of Breefs, Strangers, Carriers, & Messengers with Letters, & all others that know the name of the place, but can neither tell where it is, nor how to goe unto it. London, 1657. 4°.

— *Another edition.* London, 1662. 4°.

— *Another edition.* London, 1668. 4°.

— *Another edition.* London, 1677. 4°.

This book is a continuation of "A Direction for the English Traviller," (above, 1635–1643), with the addition of printed lists of places.

Woodhouse, John. A plaine almanack or prognostication for 1659. London, 1659. 8°.

This almanack has a range in time, so far as has been ascertained, from 1606 to 1708. It contains the fairs from 1613, but the roads are not introduced till as late as 1659. They are then fifteen in number and are copied, apparently, from Rudston's tables of 1615, perpetuating his errors in the names of places.

Ogilby, John. Britannia, Volume the First: or, an Illustration of the Kingdom of England & Dominion of Wales: By a Geographical & Historical Description of the Principal Roads thereof. Actually Ad-measured & Delineated in a Century of Whole-Sheet Copper Sculps. London, 1675. Fol.

— *Another edition.* London, 1698. Fol.

Speed, John. The Theatre of the Empire of Great-Britain. London, 1676. Fol.

In this (the last) edition of the "Theatre" are added five double-page tables of "The Principal Roads, & their Branches leading to the Cities & chief Towns in England

& Wales; with their computed distances. In a new & accurate method." These are (i) The Western Road from London to the Landsend in Cornwall; (ii) The North-West Road from London to Holyhead; (iii) The West Road from London to Bristol; (iv) The South-East, South and South-West Roads from London, and (v) The North Road from London to Berwick.

English Traveller. The English Travellers Companion: or, a Ready & Sure Guide from London to any of the Principal Cities & Towns in England & Wales. Containing all the Grand Roads with their several branches, & the Towns & Villages you pass through: To which is affixed the computed distances from one Town to another. Exhibited by Five Tables in a new & accurate Method. Very delightful for those that stay at home, & more useful for all such as have business to any part of the Kingdom. By a Lover of his Country-men. London, Printed for Tho. Basset, at the George in Fleet street; & Rich. Chiswel, at the Rose & Crown in S.t Pauls Church-yard. 1676. London, 1676. Tall, narrow 12°.

This book is made up of the five large road-maps which were added to the edition of this year of the "Theatre of the Empire of Great-Britain."

Ogilby, John. Mr. Ogilby's Tables of his Measur'd Roads. So Digested, that any great Road or Branch may readily be found; with the General & Particular, Computed & Measur'd Distance, & the Distinction of Market & Post-Towns. With other Remarks. To which is Added, a true Account of the Markets & Fairs, Etc. Collected in his Survey. By John Ogilby, Esq; His Majesty's Cosmographer. Licensed March 31th. 1676. H. Oldenburg. London, Printed by the Author, & Sold at His House in White Fryers. 1676*. London, 1676. Tall, narrow 12°.

The following "fifteen great Roads from London to the Extent of England & Wales" are given, with their branches: (i) to Aberystwyth; (ii) to Arundel; (iii) to Berwick; (iv) to Norwich; (v) to Bristol; (vi) to Hereford; (vii) to Saint David's; (viii) to Dover; (ix) to Hythe; (x) to Holyhead; (xi) to Sennen (Land's End); (xii) to Poole; (xiii) to Portsmouth; (xiv) to Rye, and (xv) to Great Yarmouth.

Playford, John. Vade Mecum, or the Necessary Companion. Containing, 1. Sir S. Morland's Perpetual Almanack, * * * 6. The

* Ogilby died in 1676.

Rates of Post-Letters, both Inland & Outland, with the Times for sending or receiving them; also the Post-Stages, shewing the Length of each Stage, & the Distance of each Post-Town from London. London, 1679. 12°.

Contains ten roads only.

— *Vade Mecum*, or, the Necessary Companion. Containing, * * * 9. The Principal Roads in England, shewing the Distance of one Town from another in measured & computed Miles, & the Distance of each from London; also the Market-Towns, on each Road with the Days of the Week the Markets are kept on; as likewise the Hundred & County each Town stands in. *Fifth edition*, with new additions. London, 1692. Tall, narrow 12°.

Contains twelve principal roads, with branches.

Falgate, Israel. Another edition. London, 1725. Tall, narrow 12°.

— *Sixteenth edition*, carefully corrected, with additions and improvements. London, 1744. Tall, narrow 12°.

Playford, John [*jun.*]. *Twenty-second edition.* London, 1772. Tall, narrow 12°.

Berry, William. The Grand Roads of England shewing all the Towns you pass thorough & in what Shire they are in with the Reputed Distance between Town & Town in Figures with a Marke for the Post-towns & Market-towns & what Day of the Week the Market is kept. London, 1679. Single sheet.

This is a diagrammatic map of the principal roads of England and Wales, from London, going as far north as Berwick, with an extension to Edinburgh.

Morgan, William. Mr. Ogilby's & William Morgan's Pocket Book of the Roads, with their Computed & Measured Distances, & the Distinction of Market & Post-Towns. The Third Impression. To which is added several Roads, & above Five hundred Market-Towns. With a Table for the ready finding any Road, City, or Market-Town, & their Distance from London. And a Sheet Map of England fitted to bind with the Book. By William Morgan, Cosmographer to Their Majesties.

London: Printed for the Author, & Christopher Wilkinson, & Sold by them at their Houses, next the Blew Boar in Ludgate-Street, & the Black Boy in Fleet-Street, & by the several Booksellers in London & Westminster. 1680. *Third edition.* London, 1680. Tall, narrow 12°.

This edition is only known from an entry in the Term Catalogues made in February, 1680. The text of the title is that of "The Fourth Impression," 1689. It is assumed that the two titles are identical. The first edition of the "Pocket-Book" is stated, in the "Advertissement" of 1689, to have been published in 1676. It may probably be the "Tables" catalogued under that date.

— *Fourth edition.* London, 1689. Tall, narrow 12°.

— *Sixth edition.* London, 1721. Tall, narrow 12°.

— *Seventh edition.* London, 1732. Square 12°.

To this edition is added "An Exact account of all the Fairs both fix't & moveable in Alphabetical Order shewing the Days on which they are held."

— *Tenth edition,* corrected. London, 1745. Square 12°.

A further addition is "A List of the Principal Trading Towns to which Letters are sent every Night from the Post-Office in London. Also the Expence of sending a Letter or Packet by Express to the most noted Towns of England."

— *Eleventh edition,* corrected and improved. London, 1752. Square 12°.

England and Wales. The Traveller's Pocket-Book: or, Ogilby & Morgan's Book of the Roads Improved & Amended, In a Method never before attempted. London, 1759. Square 12°.

— *Second edition,* corrected. London, [1761]. Square 12°.

— *Fifth edition,* corrected. London, 1770. Square 12°.

— *Sixth edition,* corrected, "With many Additions, particularly Cross Roads." London, 1771. Square 12°.

— [*Potter, John.*] *Seventeenth edition,* corrected, "With great Improvements & Additions, particularly of Cross Roads & Gentlemens Seats. By Mr. Potter, Editor of Salmon's Gazetteer." London, 1775. Square 12°.

— — *Eighteenth edition,* corrected, "With great Improvements & Additions, particularly of Cross Roads & Gentlemens Seats." London, 1777. Square 12°.

—— *Nineteenth edition*, corrected. London, 1778. Square 12°.

—— *Twentieth edition*, corrected. London, 1780. Square 12°.

— *Twenty-first edition*, corrected, and considerably improved. London, 1782. Square 12°.

— *Twenty-second edition*, corrected, and considerably improved. London, 1785. Square 12°.

— *Twenty-third edition*, corrected, and considerably improved. London, 1788. Square 12°.

— *Twenty-fourth edition*, corrected, and considerably improved. London, 1794. Square 12°.

Paterson, James. A Geographical Description of Scotland. With the Faires largely inserted; As also, an exact Table of Tides, & the Table of the Latitude & Longitude of the most remarkable places in Scotland; with other useful notes, fit for every man to know, either on Sea or Land. Exactly Calculate & formed, for the use of Travellers, Mariners, & others, who have any Affairs, or Merchandizing in this Kingdom of Scotland. By James Paterson, Mathematician. Edinburgh, 1681. 8°.

Contains a section entitled: "A Description of the most remarkable High-wayes in Scotland."

— *Third edition*, much corrected and enlarged. Edinburgh, 1687. 8°.

H., W. The Infallible Guide to Travellers, or Direct Independants. Giving a most Exact Account of the four Principal Roads of England, beginning at the Standard in Cornhill, & extending to the Sea-Shore, & branching to most of the Cities, Corporations, & Market-Towns in England & Wales, with their true distance of Miles & Furlongs, according to Mr. Oglesby's *(sic)* Dimensuration. By W. H. Gent. London, 1682. 12°.

Almanack. The City & Countrey Chapman's Almanack For the Year of our Lord 1687. Wherein all the Marts & Fairs in England, & Wales, are disposed in an Alphabetical Order in every Moneth, so that both the place where, & the day on which any of them are kept, is

immediately found. Also the Post Roads, & their several Branches
throughout England & Wales, with their Distances described in a New
Method. And the Names of all the Market Towns in every County in
England & Wales, & the day of the Week on which any of them are
kept * * * With other things useful for all sorts of Traders or
Chapmen whatsoever. London, 1686. 8°.

The following six "Post-Roads from London, with their several Stages & Branches"
are set out: The North Road; The North-West Road; The Middle-West Road; The
West Roads; The South Road, and The East Road, with six branch roads. The
almanack is published with the above title for the years 1687 to 1692.

— The Chapman's & Traveller's Almanack For the Year of Christ
1693. Wherein all the Post Roads, with their several Branches &
Distances, the Marts, Fairs, & Markets in England & Wales, are Alphabetically disposed in every Month; * * * London, 1693. 12°.

Continued with the above title for the years 1694 and 1695.

— The English Chapman's & Traveller's Almanack For the Year
of Christ, 1696. Wherein all the Post-Roads, with their several Branches
& Distances, the Marts, Fairs, & Markets in England & Wales, are
Alphabetically disposed in every Month; * * * London, 1696. 12°.

Continued for the years 1697 to 1711.

Traveller. The Traveller's Guide: or, a most exact Description of
the Roads of England. Being Mr. Ogilby's Actual Survey, & Mensuration by the Wheel, of the Great Roads to all the Considerable Cities &
Towns in England & Wales, together with the Cross-Roads from one
City or Eminent Town to another. Wherein is shewn the Distance from
Place to Place, & plain Directions given to find the Way, by setting down
every Town, Village, River, Brook, Bridge, Common, Forest, Wood,
Copse, Heath, Moor, Etc. that occur in Passing the Roads. And for the
better Illustration thereof, there are added Tables, wherein the Names
of the Places with their Distances are set down in a Column, in so plain
a manner, that a meer Stranger may Travel all over England without
any other Guide. London, 1699. 8°.

— *Another edition.* London, 1712. 8°.

Almanack. The Traveller's & Chapman's Daily Instructor: containing   * * *   The High-Ways & Roads, & how to Travel from one Place to another. The Market-Towns, & the Days of the Week whereon they are kept. London, 1705. 12°.

Twenty-three roads are set out.

Moll, Herman. Fifty Six New & Accurate Maps of Great Britain, Ireland & Wales; With All the Direct & Cross Roads exactly Tracted in the Maps,   * * *   Begun by Mr. Morden: Perfected, Corrected & Enlarg'd by Mr. Moll. London, 1708. Obl. 4°.

Contains an "Advertisement to the Reader, concerning the Use of this Book & Maps," and "A Table of the Roads treated of in this Book."

Pocket-Book. An Useful Companion: or, a Help at Hand. Being a convenient Pocket-Book. For all Gentlemen, Travellers & Traders. Containing a New Almanack,   * * *   a Description of the Roads of South & North Britain, all the Market-Towns, all the Chief Fairs: An Account of the Days of the going out, & of the Inns of all Stage-Coaches, Carriers, & Waggoners;   * * *   Rates of Hackney-Coaches, Car-men, Watermen, Oars & Tilt-Boats to Gravesend;   * * *   Together with Instructions for young Traders, in Weight, Measure & Number, & other things necessary. London, 1709. 8°.

Leland, John. The Itinerary of J. Leland publish'd   * * *   by T. Hearne. 9 vol. Oxford, 1710–12.   8°.

— The Itinerary of J. Leland. The second edition: collated & improved from the original MS. [reprinted from the edition of T. Hearne].

Second edition. 9 vol. Oxford, 1745–44. 8°.

— The Itinerary of J. Leland, the Antiquary,   * * *   published by T. Hearne.

Third edition. 9 vol. Oxford, 1770. 8°.

— The Itinerary of John Leland in or about the years 1535–43, edited by Lucy Toulmin Smith.

Another issue. 5 vol. London, 1906–10. 8°.

Scotland. A Description of the Most Remarkable High-Ways, & whole known Fairs & Mercats in Scotland, with Several other Remarkable Things: As also, a Description of the High-Ways from one Notable Town to another, over all England, & thereby how to Travel from any of them to the City of London. Edinburgh, 1711. 12°.

Britain. British Curiosities in Nature & Art; Exhibiting an Account of Natural & Artificial Rareties, both Ancient & Modern, intermixt with Historical & Geographical Passages. With a very particular Account of the Curiosities in London, & the Two Universities. And an Appendix, concerning the Posts, Markets, & their Fairs. To which is added a Scheme, containing other things most proper to be observed by Strangers, in 22 Respects, in as many Columns, curiously engraved on a Sheet to fold up. The Whole, adapted to the Use of Strangers, who may travel to see England, & for such as go thence into Foreign Parts, in order to account for what is Remarkable in their own Country; as appeareth more clearly by the Preface. London, 1713. 12°.

— British Curiosities, in Art & Nature; giving an Account of Rarities both Ancient & Modern, ∗ ∗ ∗ Likewise an Account of the Posts, Markets, & Fair-Towns. ∗ ∗ ∗ London, 1721. 12°

Differs from the preceding in the title page only.

— *Second edition*, with large additions. London, 1728. 12°.

In the three foregoing issues ten roads and other particulars are given in an appendix.

England. England Exactly Described. Or a Guide to Travellers in a Compleat Sett of Most Correct Mapps of Counties in England; being a Map for each County, wherein every Towne & Village is particularly Express'd with the Names & Limits of every Hundred & the Roads & Distances in Measured Miles according to Mr. Ogilby's Survey. Very Usefull for Gentlemen & Travellers being made fit for the pockett. Printed coloured & sold by Tho: Bakewell next yᵉ Horn-tavern in Fleet Street. London, 1716. Tall, narrow 12°.

This atlas contains four folding tables of the "Roads & Distances from London to Any Part of England & Wales; And Likewise from One Principall City to Another according to Mr. Ogilby's Account of the Computed Miles."

Gardner, Thomas. A Pocket-Guide to the English Traveller: Being a Compleat Survey & Admeasurement of all the Principal Roads & most Considerable Cross-Roads in England & Wales. In One hundred Copper-Plates. London: Printed for J. Tonson at Shakespear's Head over-against Katherine-Street in the Strand, & J. Watts at the Printing-Office in Wild-Court near Lincoln's-Inn Fields. MDCCXIX. London, 1719. 4°.

The plates follow closely in design those of John Ogilby's *Britannia,* 1675 and 1698.

Senex, John. An Actual Survey of all the Principal Roads of England & Wales; described by One Hundred Maps from Copper Plates ✳ ✳ ✳ First perform'd & publish'd by John Ogilby, Esq; and now improved, very much corrected, & made portable by John Senex. 2 vol. London, 1719. Obl. 4°.

— *Another edition.* London, 1757. Obl. 4°.

— *Another edition.* London, 1759. Obl. 4°.

— *Second edition.* London, 1762. Obl. 4°.

— *[Third edition?].* London, 1775. Obl. 4°.

Senex, John. The Roads through England delineated, or, Ogilby's Survey, Revised, Improved & Reduced to a Size portable for the Pocket By John Senex F,R,S. London, 1757. Obl. 4°.

— *Another edition.* London, 1762. Obl. 4°.

These seem to be duplicates, with a different title, of "An Actual Survey of all the Principal Roads of England & Wales" of the same dates.

England and Wales. Britannia Depicta, or Ogilby Improv'd; being a Correct Coppy of Mr. Ogilby's Actual Survey of all ye Direct & Principal Cross Roads in England & Wales: Wherein are exactly Delineated & Engraven, All ye Cities, Towns, Villages, Churches, Seats etc. scituate on or near the Roads, with their respective Distances in Measured & Computed Miles. And to render this Work universally usefull & agreeable, [beyond any of it's kind] are added in a clear & most compendious

Method—I, A full & particular Description & Account of all the Cities, Borough-Towns, Towns-Corporate etc. their Arms, Antiquity, Charters, Privileges, Trade, Rarities, etc. with suitable Remarks on all places of note drawn from the best Historians & Antiquaries. By In°. Owen of the Midd: Temple Gent. ✳ ✳ ✳ Lastly Particular & Correct Maps of all yᵉ Counties of South Britain; with a Summary Description of each County, it's Circumference, Number of Acres, Boro' & Market Towns & Parishes, Air, Soil, Comōdities, Manufacturers, & what each pays yᵉ 2ˢʰ. Aid etc. The Whole for its Compendious Variety & Exactness, preferable to all other Books of Roads hitherto Published or Proposed; And calculated not only for the direction of the Traveller [as they are] but the general use of the Gentleman & Tradesman. By Eman: Bowen Engraver. London, 1720. 8°.

— *Fourth edition*. London, 1724. 8°.

— *Another edition*. London, 1730. 8°.

— *Fourth edition*. London, 1731. 8°.

— *Another edition*. London, 1734. 8°.

— *Fourth edition*. London, 1736. 8°.

— *Fourth edition*. London, 1749. 8°.

— *Fourth edition*. London, 1751. 8°.

— *Fourth edition*. London, 1753. 8°.

— *Another edition*. London, 1755. 8°.

— *Fourth edition*. London, 1759. 8°.

— *Another edition*. London, 1764. 8°.
This last edition has a shorter and printed title.

J., G. Great Britain's *Vade Mecum*. Containing, I. A Concise Geographical Description of the World, with an Enquiry into the Nature, Quality, & Principal Commodities of each Country. II. The several Counties of England & Wales particularly Described; an Account of their valuable Products, Market Towns, Market Days, chief Fairs, Etc. * * * XI. An Account of the Roads to London from the Principal Cities & Market Towns in England & Wales; of Stage-Coaches, Waggoners, Carriers, Etc. That come to all Parts of London, Etc. their Inns, Days of coming in & going out, & the Rates & Prizes (*sic*). The whole of Universal Use to Persons of all Ranks, in Town & Country; particularly to Country Gentlemen, Travellers, Lawyers, Merchants, Tradesmen, Builders, Gaugers, Etc. By G. J. Gent. London: Printed for D. Browne, W. Mears, & F. Clay, 1720. London, 1720. Tall, narrow 12°.

Contains "An Account of the Roads to London from the Principal Cities & Market Towns in England & Wales," nineteen in number.

F., G. The Secretary's Guide. In Four Parts. * * * Part III * * * an exact Catalogue of all the Roads & Post-Stages, with the Number of Miles; * * * By G. F. Gent. London, [1720]. 12°.

— *Another issue.* London, [1734]. 12°.

This Guide contains "An exact Catalogue of all the Roads & Post-Stages in Miles & Totals, to, through, & from all the noted Places in the Kingdom of England Etc. of daily Use for all Travellers & Tradesmen, either in Coach, on Horseback, or on Foot," setting out ten roads from London.

Taylor, Thomas. The Gentlemans Pocket Companion, for Travelling into Foreign Parts: Being a most easy, plain & particular Description of the Roads from London to all the Capital Cities in Europe. With an Account of the Distances of Leagues or Miles from Place to Place, all reduced to the English Standard. Illustrated with Maps curiously engraven on Copperplates. London, 1722. 8°.

The English roads are given on the first five plates.

London and Westminster. The Foreigner's Guide: Or, a necessary & instructive Companion both for the Foreigner & Native, in their Tour through the Cities of London & Westminster. * * * III. A Description of the several Villages in the Neighbourhood * * * Also others more remote. * * * IV. An Account of the Rates of

Coaches, Watermen, Etc. Also the Rates of Post-Horses; with the Roads to Dover & Harwich. London, 1729. 8°.

Has a parallel version in French, *Le Guide des Etrangers.*

— *Another edition.* London, 1730. 8°.

— *Second edition*, corrected and improved to the present time. London, 1740. 8°.

— *Third edition*, revised, corrected and improved, and brought down to the present time. London, 1752. 8°.

— *Fourth edition*, revised and improved, with many necessary additions to the present year. London, 1763. 8°.

An English-Dutch version of this guide was also issued. Amsterdam, 1759. 8°.

Kirby, John. The Suffolk Traveller: or, a Journey through Suffolk. In which is inserted the true Distance in the Roads, from Ipswich to every Market Town in Suffolk, & the same from Bury St. Edmund's. Likewise the Distance in the Roads from one Village to another. Ipswich, 1735. 8°.

— The Suffolk Traveller. First Published by Mr. John Kirby, of Wickham-Market, who took an actual Survey of the whole County, in the Years 1732, 1733, & 1734. The Second Edition, with many Alterations & large Additions. By Several Hands. *Second edition.* London, 1764. 8°.

— [*A new edition*]. Woodbridge, [1817 c.]. 8°.

England and Wales. The Traveller's Pocket-Companion: or, a Compleat Description of the Roads, in Tables of their Computed & Measured Distances, by an actual Survey & Mensuration by the Wheel, from London to all the considerable Cities & Towns in England & Wales; together with the Mail-Roads, & their several stages, & the Cross-Roads. With Directions what Turnings are to be avoided in going or returning on Journeys, & Instructions for riding Post. By a Person who has belonged to the Publick Offices upwards of Twenty Years. London, 1741. 16°.

— The Traveller's Guide or Pocket Companion: Containing a Map of all the Direct & Cross Roads of England & Wales, according to Ogilby's Survey; shewing the distances between all the Towns situated on each Road, in Computed Miles; also the distances of the principal Market Towns from London in Measured Miles. Together with ye market Days & some Historical Remarks worthy the observation of the Curious Traveller. London, 1742. Single sheet.

A map of the roads, with printed particulars at foot, being a reprint of the road-map in "The Traveller's Pocket-Companion."

Badeslade, Thomas, and Toms, William Henry. Chorographia Britanniae, or a Set of Maps of all the Counties of England & Wales. London, 1742. 12°.

— — *Another issue.* London, 1742. 12°.

— — *Second edition.* London, 1745. 12°.

And two subsequent issues. London, no dates. 12°. Contains two "Tables of the High Roads through England & Wales," and a "Table of all the Cross Roads," with maps of the great roads from London and of the principal cross roads.

England and Wales. A New Sett of Pocket Maps of all the Counties of England & Wales ＊ ＊ ＊ Together with a Separate Map of England, a Plan of the Roads, & a Chart of the Channel. London, 1745. 4°.

This "Plan of the Roads" is a further reprint of the road-map in "The Traveller's Pocket-Companion," above.

England, Scotland and Wales. Geographia Magnae Britanniae. Or, Correct Maps of all the Counties in England, Scotland, & Wales; with General ones of both Kingdoms, & of the several Adjacent Islands: Each Map expressing the Cities, Boroughs, Market & Presbytery Towns, Villages, Roads & Rivers; with the N^o. of Members sent to Parliament; together with Tables of the high & cross Roads, market Days, Etc. 2 vol. London, 1748 & 1749. 8°.

Contains, in the first volume, 158 routes, followed by an index of the cities and market towns.

Tradesman. The Tradesman's & Traveller's Pocket Companion: or, the Bath & Bristol Guide: Calculated for the Use of Gentlemen & Ladies who visit Bath; the Inhabitants of Bath & Bristol; & all Persons who have Occasion to Travel. *Second edition*, corrected, with several additions. Bath, [1750?]. 12°.

Contains "An Exact Measure of the Roads from Bath to London, * * * as it was measured * * * in 1709."

Bath and Bristol. The Bath & Bristol Guide: or, the Tradesman's & Traveller's Pocket-Companion. Containing, * * * an exact Measurement of the Roads between Bath & London, according to the Stones erected every Mile. Bath, 1753. 12°.

— *Third edition*, with additions. Bath, [1755]. 12°.

— *Fourth edition*, with additions. Bath, [1760]. 12°.

These appear to be editions of the preceding, with slight variations in the title, etc.

England and Wales. A New & Accurate Description of the Present Great Roads & the Principal Cross Roads of England & Wales. London, 1756. 8°.

*Expilly, Jean Joseph. Le Géographe Manuel, Contenant La Description de tous les Païs du Monde, * * * leurs Villes Capitales, avec leurs distances de Paris, et les Routes qui y menent, tant par Terre que par Mer; * * * Par M. l'Abbé Expilly.* M.DCC.LVII. Paris, 1757. 18°.

— *Second edition.* Paris, 1757. 18°.

— *Third edition.* Paris, 1760. 18°.

— *Another edition.* Paris, 1761. 18°.

— *Another edition.* Paris, 1770. 18°.

— *Another edition.* Paris, 1772. 18°.

— *Another edition.* Paris, 1774. 18°.

— *A new edition,* "*avec des cartes géographiques.*" Paris, 1777. 18°.

And, entirely re-arranged by Victor Comeiras:

— *Another edition.* Paris, 1782. 18°.

— *Second edition,* "*revue et augmentée.*" Paris, 1801. 8°.

— *Another edition.* Paris, 1803. 8°.

The roads from Paris to London, to Edinburgh and to Dublin are given.

Senex, John. Les Routes d'Ogilby par l'Angleterre. Revuës, Corrigées, Augmentées, et Reduites, par Senex en 101 Cartes. Contenant un détail exact de toutes les Villes, Bourgs, Villages, Montagnes, Rivieres, Ponts, Eglises, Maisons Seigneuriales, et de tous les lieux remarquables. Bowles a ajouté en 1757 plusieurs nouvelles Routes à cet ouvrage, plusieurs renvois et corrections necessaires. Cet ouvrage a été traduit de l'Anglois par le S^r. le Rouge Ing^r. Géographe du Roy, et se vend à Paris Chez le même Rue des Grands Augustins. M.DCCLIX. Paris, 1759. Obl. 4°.

This book contains a parallel version in English. The plates are those of John Senex' "Actual Survey," of 1719, with the details on the maps re-written in French.

Bath. The New Bath Guide, or, Useful Pocket-Companion; necessary for all Persons residing at, or resorting to, this antient & opulent City. Bath, [1762]. 12°.

Contains "Measurements of the principal Coach-Roads from Bath, according to the Mile-stones, where any are erected."

— *Second edition.* Bath, [1763]. 12°.

— *Third edition.* Bath, [1764]. 12°.

— *Fourth edition.* Bath, [1766]. 12°.

— *Fifth edition.* Bath. [1768]. 12°.

Followed by issues of a *New Edition,* Bath, 12°, dated [1770], [1771], [1772], 1773, [1774], 1775, 1776, 1777, 1778, 1779, 1780, 1782, 1784, 1785, 1786, 1787, 1788, 1789, 1790, 1791, 1792, 1793, 1794, 1795, 1796, 1797, 1798, 1799, 1800, 1801, and continued, with a varied title, as:

"The Historic & Local New Bath Guide." Bath, 1801. 12°, with editions of [1805] and 1810, and again by "The Original New Bath Guide," (J. Savage), Bath, 1804. 12°, with editions of 1805, 1806, 1807, 1808, 1809; "The Improved Bath Guide" (Wood and Co.), Bath, 1809, 12°, and 1813, and "The Original Bath Guide, considerably Enlarged & Improved; comprehending Every Species of Information that can be required by the Visitor & Inhabitants" (J. Savage and Meyler and Son), Bath, 1811. 12°. Other editions 1815, 1816, 1817, 1821, 1822, 1824, 1829, 1831, 1832, 1835, 1839, 1846, and 1853 are known.

They contain an "Itinerary of the principal Roads from Bath."

Rocque, John. Rocque's Traveller's Assistant; being the Most General & Compleat Director extant, to all the Post, Principal & Cross Roads in England, Wales, Scotland & Ireland; giving the true Names & exact Distances from the Standard in Cornhill for Great-Britain; & from Dublin in Ireland, to all the several Cities, Towns, Villages, Etc, in the Three Kingdoms. The whole collected & computed in a new Manner, more clear & intelligent than any yet published. London, 1763. 12°.

Rocque, John. The Traveller's Assistant; being a General List of the Post Roads, Etc. from Cornhill, London, to the Capitals of each Empire, Kingdom, Province, Etc. in Europe. Likewise from each Capital to their respective Post Towns, Etc. Shewing the Distance in Posts, Leagues, Miles, etc. according to the different Measures made use of in each Country, agreeable to a General Map of the Post Roads of Europe, published in 1764. London, 1764. 12°.

This is published with "Rocque's Traveller's Assistant," 1763, as Vol. II.

*Michel, * * * and Desnos, L. C. L'Indicateur Fidèle, ou Guide des Voyageurs, qui enseigne Toutes les Routes Royales et Particulières de la France. * * * Contenant Toutes les Villes, Tous les Bourgs, Villages, * * * traversés par les Grandes Routes, Etc. Accompagné d'un Itinéraire Instructif et raisonné sur chaque Route, * * * Dressé par le Sieur Michel * * * Mis au Jour et Dirigé par le S^r. Desnos.* Paris, 1764. 4°.

Atlas of thirteen plates and a general map.

—— *Another edition.* Paris, 1765. 4°.

With five additional plates.

—— *Third edition, "corrigé, et considérablement augmenté en 1767."* Paris, 1766 [1767]. 4°.

—— *Third edition, "corrigé, et considérablement augmenté en 1768."* Paris, 1768. 4°.

— — *Fourth edition, "corrigé, et considérablement augmenté en* 1772." Paris, 1772. 4°.

— — *Another edition, "corrigé, et considérablement augmenté en* 1775." Paris, 1775. 4°.

— — *Fourth edition, "corrigé, et considérablement augmenté en* 1780." Paris, 1780. 4°.

— — *Fifth edition, "corrigé, et considérablement augmenté en* 1785." Paris, 1785. 4°.

Includes the south of England and the roads to London from Dover, Rye, Newhaven and Portsmouth (Sheet X).

Gibson, John. Maps of the Chief Roads in England, showing the various Routes from London. Drawn and engraved by J. Gibson. [London], 1765. Obl. 4°.

Gentleman. The Gentleman's Magazine, & Historical Chronicle. London, 1765, 1766, 1769, 1774 & 1775. 8°.

A series of plates of roads similar in style to those of Senex, eighteen in all, of which six occur in the volume for 1765, five in that for 1766, one in 1769, one in 1774 and the remaining five in the year 1775.

Knowledge and Pleasure. The Universal Magazine of Knowledge & Pleasure. London, 1765–1773. 8°.

Thirty-nine plates (preceded by a general map of the roads of England and Wales, which appeared in vol. 37, August, 1765), after Senex' reduction of John Ogilby's road-maps, run from vol. 37, October, 1765, to vol. 53, December, 1773, in this monthly magazine.

France. Nouvel Itinéraire Général, Comprenant Toutes les Grandes Routes et Chemins de communication des Provinces de France, des Isles Britanniques, et de l'Espagne, * * * *avec les Distances en Lieües ou Milles d'usage dans ces differens Pays, dressé par des auteurs connus* * * * *et publié par le S.* *Desnos.* Paris, 1766. 4°.

— *Another edition.* Paris, 1782. 4°.

An atlas of forty maps, of which four are for the British Isles.

Paterson, Daniel. A Scale of Distances of the Principal Cities & Towns of England. Giving in all 4560 distances in Measured Miles. London, 1766. Large sheet.

Senex, John. Nouvel Atlas d'Angleterre, divisé En ses 52 Comtés Avec toutes les Routes Levées Topographiquement par ordre de S.M. Britannique et les Plans des Villes et Ports de ce Royaume. A Paris. Chez le Sieur Desnos. Paris, 1767. Fol.

Another series of Senex' plates of 1719, etc,

Kitchin, Thomas. Kitchin's Post-Chaise Companion, through England & Wales; containing all the Ancient & New Additional Roads, with every Topographical Detail relating thereto. By Thomas Kitchin, For the Use of Travellers, on One Hundred & Three Copper Plates. London, 1767. Obl. 8°.

— *Another edition.* London, [1780]. Obl. 8°.

This is a further issue of Senex' plates, which appears to be the last.

Paterson, Daniel. A New & Accurate Description of all the Direct & Principal Cross Roads in Great Britain. * * * The whole on a Plan far preferable to any Work of the Kind Extant. London, 1771. 8°.

— *Second edition,* corrected. London, 1772. 8°.

— *Third edition,* corrected, and greatly improved. London, 1776. 8°

— *Fourth edition.* London, 1778. 8°.

— A New & Accurate Description of all the Direct & Principal Cross Roads in England & Wales. *Fifth edition.* London, 1781. 8°.

— *Sixth edition.* London, 1784. 8°.

— *Seventh edition.* London, 1786. 8°.

— *Eighth edition.* London, 1789. 8°.

— *Ninth edition.* London, 1792. 8°.

— *Tenth edition.* London, 1794. 8°.

— *Eleventh edition.* London, 1796. 8°.

— A New & Accurate Description of all the Direct & Principal Cross Roads in Great Britain. *Twelfth edition.* London, 1799. 8°.

Including the roads of Scotland, "which were heretofore published in a separate pamphlet," for which see under *Paterson, 1781* below.

— A New & Accurate Description of all the Direct & Principal Cross Roads in England & Wales, & part of the Roads of Scotland. *Thirteenth edition.* London, 1803. 8°.

— *Fourteenth edition.* London, 1808. 8°.

— *Fifteenth edition.* London, 1811. 8°.

— Paterson's Roads; being an entirely original & accurate description of all the Direct & Principal Cross Roads in England & Wales, with Part of the Roads of Scotland. ✳ ✳ ✳ The whole remodelled, augmented & improved. By Edward Mogg. *Sixteenth edition.* London, 1822. 8°.

— *Seventeenth edition.* London, 1824. 8°.

— *Eighteenth edition.* London, 1826. 8°.

— *Eighteenth edition.* London, 1828. 8°.

— *Eighteenth edition.* London, [1829]. 8°.

— *Eighteenth edition.* London, [1832]. 8°.

Michel, ✳ ✳ ✳ *and Desnos, L. C. Etrennes Utiles et Nécessaires aux Commerçans et Voyageurs, ou Indicateur Fidèle enseignant toutes les Routes Royales et particulières de la France, et les Chemins de Communication qui traversent les Grandes Routes;* ✳ ✳ ✳ Paris, 1771. 36°.

— *Latest edition,* "*corrigee et augm^{te} en* 1773." Paris, 1773. 36°.

— *Latest edition,* "*corrigée et augm^{te} en* 1775." Paris, 1775. 36°.

— *Latest edition,* "*corrigée et augm^{te} en* 1780." Paris, 1780. 36°.

Includes maps of the roads from Dover to London, Newhaven to London and Portsmouth to London. It appears from an advertisement in *L'Indicateur Fidèle* of 1764, that this pocket reduction for the use of travellers on horseback was first issued about that date, but no edition prior to 1771 is known to exist.

Paterson, Daniel. A Travelling Dictionary: or, Alphabetical Tables of the Distances of all the Principal Cities; Boroughs, Markets, & Sea-Port Towns in Great Britain from each other. * * * The Whole being a Second Part to the New & Accurate Description of the Roads. London, 1772. 8°.

— *Second edition.* London, 1773. 8°.

— *Third edition.* London, 1777. 8°.

— *Fourth edition*, corrected. London, 1781. 8°.

— *Fifth edition*, with great additions. London, 1787. 8°.

— *Sixth edition*, improved and corrected. London, 1792. 8°.

— *Seventh edition*, improved and corrected from the latest surveys. London, 1797. 8°.

— *Eighth edition.* London, 1799. 8°.

Bath. The Stranger's Assistant & Guide to Bath. Bath, 1773. 8°.
Contains measurements of the roads from Bath.

Jefferys, Thomas. Jefferys's Itinerary; or, Travellers Companion, through England, Wales, & Part of Scotland, containing all the Direct & Principal Cross Roads. London, 1775. Obl. 8°.

Monmouthshire and Wales. A Gentleman's Tour through Monmouthshire & Wales, In the Months of June & July, 1774. London, 1775. 12°.

Dutens, Louis. Itinéraire des Routes les plus fréquentées, ou Journal d'un Voyage aux Villes Principales de l'Europe, où l'on a marqué, en heures et minutes, le temps employé à aller d'une Poste à l'autre ; les distances en milles anglois mesurées par un Odomètre appliqué à la voiture. Paris, 1775. 8°.

— *Another edition.* Paris, 1775. 8°.

— *Another issue.* London, 1775. 8°.

— *A new edition, "augmentée d'un Voyage en Espagne."* Paris, 1777. 8°.

— *Another issue.* London, 1777. 8°.

— *Itinéraire des Routes les plus fréquentées, ou Journal d'un Voyage aux Villes Principales de l'Europe. En 1768, 1769, 1770, et 1771. A new edition.* London, 1778. 8°.

— *Itinéraire des Routes les plus fréquentées, ou Journal de plusieurs Voyages aux Villes Principales de l'Europe depuis 1768 jusqu'en 1783. Fourth edition.* Paris, 1783. 8°.

— *Fifth edition.* London, 1786. 8°.

— *Sixth edition.* Paris, 1788. 8°.

— *Another issue.* London, 1788. 8°.

— *Seventh edition, "revue, corrigée et augmentée."* Paris, 1791. 8°.

— *Sixth edition, "augmentée d'un Tour d'Angleterre."* London, 1793. 8°.

This itinerary includes roads from Edinburgh to London; from London to Paris, by way of Lille, and from London to Bath and Bristol, etc.

Kent. The Kentish Traveller's Companion, in a Descriptive View of the Towns, Villages, remarkable Buildings & Antiquities, situated on or near the Road from London to Margate, Dover & Canterbury. Canterbury and Rochester, 1776. 8°.

— *First edition.* Canterbury and Rochester, 1777. 8°.

— *Second edition,* considerably enlarged. Rochester and Canterbury, 1779. 8°.

— *Third edition,* considerably enlarged. Rochester and Canterbury, 1787. 8°.

— *Third edition,* with considerable additions. Rochester and Canterbury, 1790. 12°.

— *Fourth edition*, with considerable additions. Canterbury, 1794. 12°.

— *Fifth edition*, considerably enlarged. Canterbury, 1799. 12°.

Taylor, George, and Skinner, Andrew. Taylor & Skinner's Survey of the Great Post Roads, Between London, Bath & Bristol. London, 1776. 12°.

Taylor, George, and Skinner, Andrew. Taylor & Skinner's Survey & Maps of the Roads of North Britain, or Scotland. London, 1776. Obl. fol.

Taylor, George, and Skinner, Andrew. The Traveller's Pocket Book, or an Abstract of Taylor & Skinner's Survey of the Roads of Scotland. London, 1776. 24°.

Armstrong, Mostyn John. An Actual Survey of the Great Post-Roads between London & Edinburgh. With the Country Three Miles, on each Side, Drawn on a Scale of Half an Inch to a Mile. London, 1776. 8°.

— *Second edition.* London, 1783. 8°.

Armstrong, Mostyn John. Armstrong's Actual Survey of the Great Post Road between London & Dover, With the Country Three Miles on each Side. Drawn on a Scale of Half an Inch to a Mile. London, 1777. 8°.

Has a parallel title in French, *Une Vue Actuelle de la Grande Route de Poste depuis Londres jusqu'à Douvres.*

[*Cradock, Joseph.*] Letters from Snowdon: Descriptive of a Tour through the Northern Counties of Wales. Containing the Antiquities, History, & State of the Country: With the Manners & Customs of the Inhabitants. The Second Edition. To which is added an Account of the Inns & Roads, with Directions for Travellers. *Second edition.* London, 1777. 12°.

The first edition, London, 1770, 12°, has no particulars of the roads.

West, Thomas. A Guide to the Lakes: dedicated to the Lovers of Landscape Studies, & to all who have visited, or intend to visit the Lakes in Cumberland, Westmorland, & Lancashire. By the Author of the Antiquities of Furness. London, 1778. 8°.

Includes the roads from Lancaster to the Lake district.

— A Guide to the Lakes, in Cumberland, Westmorland, & Lancashire. *Second edition,* revised throughout and greatly enlarged. London, 1780. 8°.

— *Third edition.* London, 1784. 8°.

— *Fourth edition.* London, 1789. 8°.

— *Fifth edition.* London, 1793. 8°.

— *Sixth edition.* London, 1796. 8°.

— *Seventh edition.* London, 1799. 8°.

— *Eighth edition.* Kendal, 1802. 8°.

— *Ninth edition.* Kendal, 1807. 8°.

— *Tenth edition.* Kendal, 1812. 8°.

— *Eleventh edition.* Kendal, 1821. 8°.

— *Another edition.* Carlisle, [1833]. 12°.

Great Britain. The Modern Universal British Traveller; or, A New, Complete, & Accurate Tour through England, Wales, Scotland, & the Neighbouring Islands. ✳ ✳ ✳ And including ✳ ✳ ✳ A Complete Road-Book; a List of all the Fairs, & a Variety of other useful & entertaining Particulars. London, 1779. Fol.

Owen, William. Owen's New Book of Roads: or, a Description of the Roads of Great Britain. Being a Companion to Owen's Complete Book of Fairs. *Second edition,* corrected and greatly improved. London, 1779. 12°.

— *Third edition.* London, 1782. 12°.

— *Fourth edition.* London, 1784. 12°.

— *Fifth edition.* London, 1788. 12°.

— *Seventh edition.* London, 1796. 12°.

— *Eighth edition.* London, 1799. 12°.

— *Another edition.* London, 1802. 12°.

— *A new edition.* London, 1805. 12°.

— *A new edition.* London, 1808. 12°.

— *A new edition.* London, 1814. 12°.

— *A new edition.* London, 1817. 12°.

— *A new edition.* London, 1822. 12°.

— *A new edition.* London, 1827. 12°.

— *Another edition.* London, 1840. 12°.

It is probable that the first edition is of even date with "Owen's Book of Fairs," the 6th edition, London, 1774, 12°. Of the "Book of Fairs" the following editions are known: 1756, 1774, 1783, 1784, 1788, 1792, 1799, 1802, 1813, 1817 [1856 and 1859 (J. Donaldson)].

Tunbridge Wells. The Tunbridge Wells Guide; or An Account of the ancient & present State of that Place, To which is Added a particular Description of the Towns & Villages, Gentlemens Seats, Remains of Antiquity, Founderies, Etc. Etc. within the Circumference of Sixteen Miles. Tunbridge Wells, Printed & Sold by J. Sprange. 1780. 8°.

At the end: "Useful Roads, leading from Tunbridge-Wells, described."

— *Another issue.* Tunbridge Wells, 1785. 8°.

— *Another issue.* Tunbridge Wells, 1786. 8°.

— *Another issue.* Tunbridge Wells, 1787. 8°.

— *Another issue.* Tunbridge Wells, 1796. 8°.

— *Another issue.* Tunbridge Wells, 1797. 8°.

— *Another issue.* Tunbridge Wells, 1800. 8°.

— *Another issue.* Tunbridge Wells, 1801. 8°.

— *Another issue.* Tunbridge Wells, 1806. 8°.

— *Another issue.* Tunbridge Wells, 1809. 8°.

— *Another issue.* Tunbridge Wells, 1811. 8°.

— *Another issue.* Tunbridge Wells, 1815. 8°.

— *Another issue.* Tunbridge Wells, 1817. 8°.
Continued with the same title: "Printed & Published by J. Clifford."

— *Another issue.* Tunbridge Wells, 1817. 8°.
Continued as:

— A Descriptive Guide of Tunbridge Wells & its environs; in which is delineated every particular interesting to the visitor & resident. Embellished with an Accurate Map of the Roads round the place. Tunbridge Wells, 1818. 8°.

— *Second edition.* Tunbridge Wells, 1821. 8°.

— *Second edition.* Tunbridge Wells, 1822. 8°.

— *Third edition.* Tunbridge Wells, 1823. 8°.

— *Fourth edition.* Tunbridge Wells, 1828. 8°.

— *Fifth edition.* Tunbridge Wells, 1829. 8°.

— *Sixth edition.* Tunbridge Wells, 1834. 8°.

— *Seventh edition.* Tunbridge Wells, 1837. 8°.

— *Seventh edition,* revised. Tunbridge Wells, 1840. 8°.

— *Eighth edition.* Tunbridge Wells, 1843. 8°.

Brighton. A Description of Brighthelmston, & the Adjacent Country; or the New Guide for Ladies & Gentlemen using that Place of Health & Amusement. London, [1780]. 12°.

— *Another edition.* Brighton, [1783]. 12°.

— *Another edition.* Brighton, [1788]. 12°.

— *Another edition.* London, [1792]. 12°.

— *Another edition.* Brighton, 1794. 12°.

— *Another edition.* Brighton, 1795. 12°.

— *Another edition.* London, 1800. 12°.

— *Another edition.* London, [1801]. 8°.

Paterson, Daniel. A New & Accurate Description of all the Direct & Principal Cross Roads of Scotland. *Fifth edition,* corrected and improved, with additions. London, 1781. 8°.

— *Sixth edition.* London, 1791. 8°.

The four earlier impressions are found in the first four issues of Paterson's "Roads in Great Britain," 1771, 1772, 1776 and 1778, in the twelfth edition of which, 1799, and thereafter, the roads of Scotland are again incorporated.

Bowles, Carrington. Bowles's Post-Chaise Companion; or, Travellers Directory through England & Wales; Being an Actual Survey of all the Principal, Direct, & Cross Roads, both Ancient & Modern; with the Distances expressed in single Miles according to Measurement: Exhibiting the several Towns, Villages, Post-Stages, etc. on or near the Roads. 2 vol. London, no date. 8°.

— *Second edition.* 2 vol. London, 1782. 8°.

Highmore, John. Journal of Travels made through the Principal Cities of Europe: Wherein the Time employed in going from Post to Post is marked in Hours & Minutes; the Distances in English Miles, measured by Means of a Perambulator fastened to the Chaise; * * * Together with an Account of the best Inns, etc. * * * Translated from the French of M. L. Dutens * * * By John Highmore, Gent. London, 1782. 8°.

— *Another edition.* London, 1792. 8°.

This is a translation of Louis Dutens' *Itinéraire,* Paris and London, 1775, etc.

Kitchin, Thomas. The Traveller's Guide through England & Wales, containing I. The route from stage to stage through the direct High Roads leading from London to all parts of the Kingdom. II. The direct roads across the country, etc. London, 1783. 4°.

Moreau, Simeon. A Tour to Cheltenham Spa; or Gloucestershire Display'd. Containing, an Account of Cheltenham, * * * With a Correct Itinerary from Cheltenham. Bath, 1783. 12°.

— *Second edition.* Bath, 1786. 12°.

— *Third edition.* Bath, 1788. 12°.

With the addition in the title of: "And an Account of the Posts from Gloucester & Cheltenham."

— *Fourth edition.* Bath, 1789. 12°.

— *Fifth edition.* Bath, 1789. 12°.

— *Seventh edition.* Bath, 1793. 12°.

— *Eighth edition.* Bath, 1797. 12°.

— *Ninth edition.* Bath, 1797. 12°.

— *Another edition.* Bath, 1805. 12°.

Cary, John. Cary's Actual Survey, of the Great Post Roads between London & Falmouth, including a Branch to Weymouth, as well as those from Salisbury to Axminster, either thro' Dorchester or Sherborne; those from Basingstoke to Salisbury, either thro' Popham Lane or Andover; & those from Exeter to Truro, either thro' Plymouth or Launceston, wherein every Gentleman's Seat, Village, Town, Etc. within sight of the Road, is laid down, the principal Inns on the Road expressed, & the exact Distances ascertained, By A. Arrowsmith Land Surveyor. 1782. London, 1784. 12°.

Paterson, Daniel. Paterson's British Itinerary, Being a new & accurate Delineation & Description of the Direct & Principal Cross Roads of Great Britain. 2 vol. London, 1785. 8°.

— *Second edition*, improved. 2 vol. London, 1796. 8°.

— *Second edition*, improved. 2 vol. London, 1803. 8°.

— *Second edition*, improved. 2 vol. London, 1807. 8°.

Italy. Nuova Descrizione di tutte le Città di Europa, * * * *Con le distanze di tutte le Poste, e tariffe di quello si deve pagare.* * * * *In Roma* MDCCLXXXV. Rome, 1785. 12°.

Contains the road from Paris to London, with short descriptions of Canterbury, Rochester and London.

Cambridge. A Concise & Accurate Description of the University, Town & County of Cambridge: * * * To which is added an exact Account of the Roads, Posts, Coaches, Diligences, Stage-Waggons, Etc. *A new and improved edition.* Cambridge, [1785]. 12°.

The earlier issues, headed on title: "*Cantabrigia Depicta,*" have no road-tables.

— *A new edition*, corrected and enlarged. Cambridge, [1790]. 12°.

Continued as:

— A Description of the University, Town, & County of Cambridge: containing * * * Directions concerning the Posts, Roads, Stage Coaches, Waggons, Etc. to & from Cambridge. Cambridge, 1796. 12°.

— *Another edition.* Cambridge, 1797. 12°.

— *Another edition.* Cambridge, 1799. 12°.

— *Another edition.* Cambridge, 1801. 12°.

And further continued as:

— A Guide through the University of Cambridge: containing * * * a Description of the Town, County, & Neighbourhood of Cambridge. *A new edition*, considerably enlarged. Cambridge, [1803]. 12°.

— *Another edition.* Cambridge, [1804]. 12°.

— *Another edition.* Cambridge, [1807]. 12°.

— *Another edition.* Cambridge, 1808. 12°.

— *A new edition*, considerably enlarged. Cambridge, 1811. 12°.

— *A new edition*, considerably enlarged. Cambridge, [1812]. 12°.

— *A new edition*, considerably enlarged. Cambridge, 1814. 12°.

— *A new edition*, considerably enlarged. Cambridge, [1815]. 12°.

— *A new edition*, considerably improved. Cambridge, 1820. 12°.

— The Cambridge Guide, or, a Description of the University & Town of Cambridge. *A new edition*, revised and corrected. Cambridge, [1830]. 12°.

— *A new edition*. Cambridge, 1837. 12°.

— The Cambridge Guide, including Historical & Architectural Notices of the Public Buildings. *A new edition*. Cambridge, 1838. 12°.

— *A new edition*. Cambridge, 1845. 12°.

Cary, John. Cary's Actual Survey of the Country Ten Miles round Hampton Court & Richmond; On a Scale of one Inch to a Mile. Wherein the Roads, Rivers, Woods & Commons; as well as every Market Town, Village Etc. are distinguished; & every Seat shewn with the Name of the Possessor. London, 1786. 8°.

Cary, John. Cary's Actual Survey of the Country Fifteen Miles round London. On a Scale of one Inch to a Mile. Wherein the Roads, Rivers, Woods & Commons; as well as every Market Town, Village Etc. are distinguished; & every Seat shewn with the Name of the Possessor. London, 1786. 8°.

— *Another issue.* London, 1800. 8°.

— *Another issue.* London, 1811. 8°.

Tunnicliff, William. A Topographical Survey of the Counties of Stafford, Chester & Lancaster, containing a new-engraved Map of each County, with a complete Description of the Great, Direct, & Cross Roads; * * * To which is added, The Direction & Survey of the Great Roads, * * * By William Tunnicliff, Land-Surveyor. Nantwich, 1787. 8°.

— *Another issue*, with the addition of the Counties of Somerset, Gloucester and Worcester. Bath, 1789. 8°.

Love, John. The New Waymouth Guide; or, Useful Pocket Companion: containing a Description of Waymouth, * * * Also the Distances from Waymouth, to the Principal Watering Places; & an Alphabetical List of the Cities & Market Towns in Great Britain, measured from thence. Weymouth, [1788]. 8°.

Pride, Thomas, and Luckombe, Philip. The Traveller's Companion; or New Itinerary of England & Wales, with part of Scotland; arranged in the manner of Copper-plates, being An Accurate & Comprehensive View of the Principal Roads in Great Britain, taken from Actual Surveys; Wherein every Object worthy of Notice is pointed out. London, 1789. 8°.

Jung, Philippe. Guide d'Oxford: avec un Catalogue de tout ce qu'il y a de plus remarquable dans toute la Province d'Oxford: avec la Route de Douvres à Londres, les deux Routes de Londres à Oxford, et les objets remarquables, que l'on y apperçoit. Oxford, 1789. 12°.

Bott, W. A Description of Buxton, & the Adjacent Country; or the New Guide, for Ladies and Gentlemen, Resorting to that Place of Health & Amusement. Manchester, 1790. 12°.

— *Another edition.* Manchester, 1792. 12°.

— *Another edition.* Manchester, 1795. 12°.

— *Another edition.* Manchester, 1796. 12°.

— *Fourth edition.* Manchester, 1800. 12°.

— *Sixth edition.* Manchester, 1803. 12°.

— *Eighth edition.* Sheffield, no date. 12°.

— A Description of Buxton & the Adjacent Country, In which will be found a correct Guide & Directory to all the romantic & charming scenes of that Salubrious Village & its Vicinity; with an accurate statement of the many virtues of its Medicinal Waters. *Tenth edition.* Macclesfield, 1813. 12°.

— *Eleventh edition.* Manchester, 1818. 12°.

Contains the "Measurement of the Principal Post Roads from Buxton, according to the mile stones."

Cary, John. Cary's Survey of the High Roads from London to Hampton Court, Bagshot, Oakingham, [& 23 other places in the neighbourhood of the Metropolis.] On a Scale of one Inch to a Mile; Wherein every Gentleman's Seat, situate on, or seen from the Road, (however distant) are laid down, with the Name of the Possessor; to which is added the Number of Inns on each separate Route; also, The different Turnpike Gates, shewing the Connection which one Trust has with another. London, 1790. 4°.

— *Another issue.* London, 1799. 4°.

— *Another issue.* London, 1801. 4°.

— *Another issue.* London, 1810. 4°.

Cary, John. Cary's Traveller's Companion, or, a Delineation of the Turnpike Roads of England & Wales; shewing the immediate Rout[e] to every Market & Borough Town throughout the Kingdom. Laid down from the best Authorities, on a New Set of County Maps. London, 1790. 8°.

— *Another issue.* London, 1791. 8°.

— *Another issue.* London, 1806. 8°.

— *Another issue.* London, 1810. 8°.

— *Another issue.* London, 1812. 8°.

— *Another issue.* London, 1814. 8°.

— *Another issue.* London, 1817. 8°.

— *Another issue.* London, 1819. 8°.

— *Another issue.* London, 1821. 8°.

— *Another issue.* London, 1822. 8°.

— *Another issue.* London, 1824. 8°.

— *Another issue.* London, 1826. 8°.

— *Another issue.* London, 1828. 8°.

There are four states of the issue of 1791, and two each of those of 1806, 1814 and 1819.

Tunnicliff, William. A Topographical Survey of the Counties of Hants, Wilts, Dorset, Somerset, Devon, & Cornwall; Commonly called the Western Circuit, containing an accurate & comprehensive Description of all the Principal Direct & Cross Roads in each respective County. In which the Situation of all the Towns, Villages, Noblemen's & Gentlemen's Seats, Navigable Rivers, Canals, Etc. upon & in the Vicinity of each Road, are particularly expressed, & their relative Distances exactly ascertained. Salisbury, 1791. 8°.

Cary, John. The Road from the New Port of Milford; to the New Passage of the Severn, & Gloucester; Survey'd in the Year 1790 by C. Hassall, of Eastwood, Pembroke-shire, & J. Williams of Margam, Glamorgan-shire, by order of the South Wales Association for the Improvement of Roads. London, 1792. 8°.

Robertson, Archibald. A Topographical Survey of the Great Road from London to Bath & Bristol. With Historical & Descriptive Accounts, of the Country, Towns, Villages, & Gentlemen's Seats on & adjacent to it. 2 part. London, 1792. 8°.

Gloucester. The Gloucester Guide; being a brief and methodical account of Every Thing that is Worthy of Observation, in that Ancient City, Suburbs, &c. * * * To which is added an Appendix, with an Account of the Neighbouring Roads. * * * Collected & arranged by a Citizen, & Member of the University of Oxford. London, 1792. 12°.

Holyhead. The Traveller's Companion, from Holyhead, to London. London, 1793. 12°.

Brighton. Brighton New Guide; or, a Description of Brighthelmston & the adjacent country. London, 1794. 12°.

Contains tables of roads, with distances, from Brighton to London, Tunbridge Wells, Margate, Portsmouth, Southampton and Bath and Bristol.

— *Another edition.* London, 1800. 12°.

— *Fourth edition.* London, no date. 12°.

— Fisher's New Brighton Guide; or, a Description of Bright-helmston, & the adjacent Country. *Sixth edition*, with additions. London, 1804. 8°.

Edinburgh. The Traveller's Companion through the City of Edin-burgh & Suburbs. Edinburgh, 1794. 8°.

Contains a "General List of the Post Roads through Scotland in Miles from Edinburgh."

Inhabitant. The Hastings' Guide; or, a Description of that Ancient Town & Port & its Environs; ＊ ＊ ＊ with a Table of Distances from Hastings to the Places Adjacent. London, 1794. 8°.

— *Second edition.* London, 1797. 8°.

— *Third edition.* London, 1804. 8°.

— *Fourth edition.* London, 1815. 8°.

— *Fifth edition.* Hastings, [1820]. 8°.

Baker, James. A Picturesque Guide through Wales & the Marches; interspersed with the most interesting subjects of Antiquity in that Principality*. *Second edition*, with considerable alterations and additions. 3 vol. Worcester, 1795. 4°.

Scarborough. The Scarborough Guide (A Second Edition). To which is prefixed, a Descriptive Route through Hull & Beverley, with occa-sional Remarks, Anecdotes, & Characters. Hull, 1796. 8°.

Cary, John. Cary's New Itinerary; or, An Accurate Delineation of the Great Roads, both Direct & Cross, throughout England & Wales; With many of the principal Roads in Scotland. From an Actual Ad-measurement made by Command of His Majesty's Postmaster General. London, 1798. 8°.

＊ As to the various titles and dates of this curious publication see "An Artist Topo-grapher" by John Ballinger. (Reprinted from "The Library," April, 1916). London, 1916. 8°.

— *Another issue.* London, 1798. 8°.

— *Second edition.* London, 1802*. 8°.

— *Third edition.* London, 1806. 8°.

— *Fourth edition.* London, 1810. 8°.

— *Fifth edition.* London, 1812. 8°.

— *Sixth edition.* London, 1815. 8°.

— *Seventh edition.* London, 1817. 8°.

— *Eighth edition.* London, 1819. 8°.

— *Ninth edition.* London, 1821. 8°.

— *Tenth edition.* London, 1826. 8°.

— *Eleventh edition.* London, 1828. 8°.

Besides the two issues of 1798, there are two states of each of the following editions: 5th, 6th, 7th and 9th and three of that of 1810 (4th).

Scotland. The Traveller's Guide; or A Topographical Description of Scotland, & of the Islands belonging to it. Edinburgh, 1798. 8°.

Contains "A Table of the Stages, & a description of the principal Roads."

— The Traveller's Guide through Scotland & It's Islands. *Fourth edition.* Edinburgh, 1808. 8°.

— The Traveller's Guide through Scotland & its Islands. Illustrated by maps, sketches of Pleasure Tours, views of remarkable buildings, & a plan of the Lakes of Cumberland. *Fifth edition.* Edinburgh, 1811. 8°.

— *Sixth edition.* 2 vol. Edinburgh, 1814. 8°.

— *Seventh edition.* 2 vol. Edinburgh, 1818. 8°.

— The Traveller's Guide through Scotland. Illustrated by Maps,

* In the early part of the nineteenth century innkeepers on the great post roads were in the habit of printing, on the backs of their bills, tables of roads and distances, with the names of the inns and of their proprietors. Other such tables appeared at this period in local almanacks. Of these trifling and ephemeral publications some few specimens have survived, in consequence of their having been pasted, or left loose, in the road-books in common use, in the same way as are found occasionally in these books turnpike-gate tickets, now become a curiosity.

views of remarkable buildings, Etc. With an Itinerary. *Eighth edition.* 2 vol. Edinburgh, 1824. 8°.

"To this edition has been added an Account of the Roads, on a plan at once novel, clear, & intelligible, after the method of Mogg's Edition of Paterson's Roads in England."

— The Traveller's Guide through Scotland, with accurate maps, views, Etc. Ninth Edition, with an Itinerary on a new plan. *Ninth edition.* Edinburgh, 1828. 8°.

— *Ninth edition.* Edinburgh, 1829. 8°.

Richardson, T. Guide to Loch Lomond, Loch Long, Loch Fine, & Inverary, with actual survey by T. Richardson, Geographer & Surveyor. With a concise description of all the Towns, Villages, Gentlemen's Seats, Etc. situated near these Roads. Glasgow, 1798. 12°.

Warner, Richard. A Walk through Wales, in August 1797, By the Rev^d. Richard Warner, of Bath. Bath, 1798. 8°.

— *Second edition.* Bath, 1798. 8°.

— *Third edition.* Bath, 1799. 8°.

Warner, Richard. A Second Walk through Wales, By the Rev^d. Richard Warner, of Bath, in August & September 1798. Bath, 1799. 8°.

— *Second edition.* Bath, 1800. 8°.

Scotland. The Direct & Principal Cross Roads of Scotland. Edinburgh, 1799. 8°.

Coltman, Nathaniel. The British Itinerary, or Traveller's Pocket Companion throughout Great Britain. Exhibiting the Direct Roads to every Borough & Commercial Town in the Kingdom. With the principal Cross Roads. Compiled from Actual Measurement & the best Surveys & Authorities. By Nathan^l. Coltman, Surveyor. London: 1st July 1799. London, 1799. 24°

Bingley, William. A Tour round North Wales, performed during the Summer of 1798. 2 vol. London, 1800. 8°.

Smith, Charles. Smith's Actual Survey of the Roads from London to Brighthelmstone, Through Ryegate, Crawley & Cuckfield, with a branch to Worthing. Also from London to Worthing, through Dorking, Horsham & Steyning, with a branch from Steyning to Brighthelmstone. London, 1800. 12°.

Warner, Richard. A Walk through some of the Western Counties of England. By the Rev^d. Richard Warner, of Bath. Bath, 1800. 8°.

Ryall, J. Ryall's New Weymouth Guide, containing a Description of Weymouth. Weymouth, [1800]. 8°.

Contains "Useful Roads, with the Distances in Measured Miles from Weymouth," and "Distances in Measured Miles, from Weymouth, to the Cities & Principal Market Towns in Great Britain."

Edwards, J. A Companion from London to Brighthelmston, in Sussex; consisting of a Set of Topographical Maps from Actual Surveys, on a Scale of Two Inches to a Mile. With Ichnographical Plans of some of the principal Towns within the Circuit of the said Survey, Picturesque Views of Seats, & a variety of elucidating Engravings, executed by Artists of the first Eminence. A complete & comprehensive Description, Natural History, & Antiquities, of all the Towns, Villages, Gentlemen's Seats, Etc. on the Road & circumjacent Country from London to Brighthelmston. & an Account of the Inns where Post-Chaises & Post-Horses are kept; Stage Coaches, Stage Waggons, & other Vehicle Inns; with their usual Hours of passing to & from London. Also a correct List of the principal Professions, noted Manufactories, principal Academies, Etc. Etc. To which are prefixed, *Tabulae Distantiarum*; ✱ ✱ ✱ By J. Edwards, Topographer. London, 1801. Large 4°.

Evans, Thomas. Cambrian Itinerary, or Welsh Tourist, ✱ ✱ ✱ illustrated by a new & correct Map of the Principality, including the roads, rivers & mountains. London, 1801. 12°.

Reissued as :

— Walks through Wales; containing a Topographical & Statistical description of the Principality: To which is prefixed a copious Travelling Guide, exhibiting the Direct & Principal Cross Roads, Inns, Distances of Stages, & Noblemen & Gentlemen's Seats. [*Second edition.*] London, 1819. 12°.

The text of the above is identical with that of the Welsh sections of "The Modern British Traveller" of [1802?–1810?].

Kearsley, George. Kearsley's Traveller's Entertaining Guide through Great Britain; or, a Description of the Great & Principal Cross-Roads; marking the distances of places from London, & from each other. London, 1801. 8°.

— *Second edition*, much enlarged and improved. London, 1803. 8°.

In this edition is added a "Description of the principal Great Roads of Ireland; Different Routes to Paris," etc.

Germany. Allgemeines Post- und Reisebuch von Deutschland und dessen angrenzenden Laendern. Frankfort, 1801. 12°.

— *Another edition.* Frankfort, 1819. 12°.

Contains roads in England: (i) Dover to London; (ii) Harwich to London; (iii) Yarmouth to London; (iv) London to Falmouth and to Plymouth; (v) London to Edinburgh; (vi) London to Dublin; (vii) London to Oxford; (viii) London to Birmingham, and (ix) London to Manchester. There is a French version of this road-book.

Evans, John. Circular Tour from Chester through North Wales. London, 1802. 32°.

Baker, James. The Imperial Guide, with Picturesque Plans of the Great Post Roads, containing Miniature Likenesses, engraved from real sketches, of the cities, towns, villages, seas, islands, mountains, public edifices, & private buildings, situated in & near such thoroughfares. London, 1802– . 8°.

Vol. 1 only published.

[*Baker, James.*] Multum in Parvo. Fashionable Tours, from London to the pleasant parts of Lancashire, Yorkshire, Westmoreland, Cumberland, Etc. Etc. & the Northern Coast of Wales, as far as Holyhead. London, 1802. 12°.

Gloucester. The Gloucester New Guide * * * together with a Directory * * * also the Different Routes & Roads through the County. Gloucester, 1802. 8°.

Paris. A Practical Guide during a Journey from London to Paris; with a correct Description of all the objects deserving notice in the French Metropolis. London, 1802. 24°.

Contains tables of four routes from London to Paris, as used at that period, namely: (i) by Dover, Calais and Amiens; (ii) by Margate, Ostend and Lille; (iii) by Harwich and Rotterdam, and (iv) by Brighton and Dieppe.

Cooke, George Alexander. The Modern British Traveller, or, Tourist's Pocket Dictionary. Being an accurate history & description of all the Counties in England, Scotland & Wales. 47 vol. London, [1802?–1810?]. 12°.

To each volume is prefixed, "A Copious Travelling Guide; Exhibiting, The Direct & principal Cross Roads Inns & Distance of Stages, Noblemen's & Gentlemen's Seats. Forming a Complete County Itinerary." There are numerous reprints, generally undated, up to as late as about 1830.

Cary, John. Cary's British Traveller; or, An abridged edition of his New Itinerary: Containing the whole of the Roads, Direct or Cross, throughout England & Wales; with many of the principal roads of Scotland: As described in his larger Work, * * * Calculated for the Use of those Travellers by whom the Gentlemen's Seats may not be considered essential. London, 1803. 8°.

Scotland. The Gazetteer of Scotland: Containing a Particular & Concise Description of the Counties, Parishes, Islands, Cities, Towns, Villages, Lakes, Rivers, Mountains, Valleys, Etc. of that Kingdom. Dundee, 1803. 8°.

In an appendix, "Principal Roads of Scotland."

— Gazetteer of Scotland; containing a Particular Description of the Counties, Parishes, Islands, Cities, Towns, Villages, Lakes, Rivers, Mountains, Vallies, Etc. in that Kingdom: with * * * A Correct Table of the Principal Roads. *Second edition*, corrected and enlarged. Edinburgh, 1806. 8°.

Wallis, James. Wallis's Pocket Itinerary. Being a New & Accurate Guide to all the principal Direct & Cross Roads throughout England, Wales & Scotland. London, 1803. 12°.

Lancaster. Sketch of a Tour from Lancaster, round the Principal Lakes in Lancashire, Cumberland, & Westmorland. Carlisle, 1803. 12°.

Ruff, H. The History of Cheltenham and its Environs. Cheltenham, 1803. 8°.

Feltham, J. A Guide to all the Watering & Sea-Bathing Places; with a Description of the Lakes; a Sketch of a Tour in Wales; & Itineraries. London, [1803]. 12°.

— *Another edition.* London, 1808. 12°.

— *A new and improved edition.* London, [1810]. 12°.

— *Another edition.* London, [1812]. 12°.

— *Another edition.* London, 1815. 12°.

— *Another edition.* London, [1824]. 12°.

— *Another edition.* London, [1825]. 12°.

England. An Atlas of England. London, [1803 *c.*]. 8°.

Contains "A Description of the Principal Post Roads in England," and "An Alphabetical List of all Cities, Townes, & Villages, in England & Wales, with the distances from London."

Ogilvy, David, jun. A General Itinerary of England & Wales, with part of Scotland; containing all the Direct & Principal Cross Roads to every City & Market Town * * * Arranged on a New Plan. London, 1804. 8°.

England. Description géographique, topographique, pittoresque, industrielle et commerciale de l'Angleterre, de l'Ecosse et de l'Irlande, * * * par Crutwell, traduite de l'anglais sur la 4ᵉ édition, avec un itinéraire de la Grande Bretagne, * * * Traduit de l'anglais de Kearsley. 4 vol. London, 1804. 18°.

Paterson, Daniel. Paterson's Roads in a pocket Size for the convenience of Travellers on Horseback, being a New & Accurate Description of all Direct & Principal Cross Roads in England & Wales, & part of Scotland. London, 1804. 8°.

No copy of this work is known to exist. The above title is taken from the entry at Stationers' Hall, by Francis Newbery, May 3rd, 1804.

Bingley, William. North Wales; including its Scenery, Antiquities, Customs, & some Sketches of its Natural History; delineated from two excursions through all the interesing parts of that Country, during the Summers of 1798 & 1801. 2 vol. London, 1804. 8°.

— North Wales, delineated from Two Excursions through all the interesting parts of that highly beautiful & romantic country, & intended as a Guide to future Tourists. *Second edition.* London, 1814. 8°.

A third edition of this book, with a title again varied, was published, after the death of the author, by his son, W. R. Bingley (London, 1839. 8°), but in this edition all road-book particulars are omitted.

Duncan, James. The Scotch Itinerary, containing the Roads through Scotland, on a New Plan. With copious observations for the Instruction & Entertainment of Travellers. And a Complete Index. Glasgow, 1805. 12°.

— The Scotch Itinerary, containing the Roads through Scotland, on a New Plan. With copious observations for the entertainment of Travellers. With two complete indexes, & an appendix. *Second edition,* corrected, improved and enlarged. Glasgow, 1808. 12°.

— Duncan's Itinerary of Scotland; containing the Roads through Scotland, & the principal roads to London; * * * With an appendix. *Third edition,* corrected and much improved. Glasgow, 1816. 12°.

— Duncan's Itinerary of Scotland; with the Principal Roads to London, copious observations on each road, & an appendix. *Fourth edition*, with important alterations. Glasgow, 1820. 12°.

— *Fifth edition*, with important alterations. Glasgow, 1823. 12°.

— *Sixth edition*, with important alterations and additions. Glasgow, 1827. 12°.

— *Seventh edition*, with important alterations and additions. Glasgow, [1830?]. 12°.

Evans, John. Picture of Worthing; to which is added an Account of Arundel & Shoreham, with other parts of the surrounding country. London, 1805. Sm. 8°.

Taylor, George, and Skinner, Andrew. Taylor & Skinner's Survey of the Roads of Scotland, on an Improved Plan. To which is prefixed an accurate Map of Scotland, with the New Roads, Etc. Etc. since the survey was taken. Edinburgh, [1805]. 8°.

— — *Another edition.* Edinburgh, [1813]. 8°.
This is a reduction of the "Survey & Maps," of 1776.

Carnarvon. A Short Account of Caernarvon, & Bedd-Kill-Hart, or, Beddgelart, Etc. Carnarvon, 1806. 12°.
Contains an itinerary of eleven pages.

Coltman, Nathaniel. Laurie & Whittle's New Traveller's Companion. Exhibiting a Complete & Correct Survey of all the Direct & Principal Cross Roads in England, Wales, & Scotland, as far North as Edinburgh & Glasgow. London, 1806. 8°.

— *Fourth edition*, corrected to 1810. London, [1810]. 8°.

— *Fifth edition*, improved. London, 1810. 8°.

— *Another edition.* London, 1811. 8°.

— *Sixth edition*, corrected and greatly improved. [With an Index Villaris.] London, 1812. 8°.

— *Seventh edition.* London, 1813. 8°.

— *Seventh edition.* [Whittle and Laurie.] London, 1814. 8°.

— Laurie's Traveller's Companion: Exhibiting a Complete & Correct Survey of all the Direct & Principal Cross Roads in England, Wales, & Scotland: as far North as Edinburgh & Glasgow: together with the Roads to Perth & Aberdeen, Greenock, Irvine, Ayr, Port-Patrick, Wigton, Etc. Accompanied by a New General Map, which exhibits the whole at one view; & an Index Villaris. *Ninth edition*, corrected and greatly improved. London, 1824. 8°.

— Laurie's New Traveller's Companion, & Guide through the Roads of England & Wales, including great part of Scotland; with a General Map, & an Index Villaris, Etc. *An improved edition*, corrected to the present time. London, 1828. 8°.

— *Another edition.* London, 1830. 8°.

— *Another edition.* London, 1834. 8°.

— *An improved edition*, corrected to the present time. London, 1836. 8°.

Cheltenham. The Historic & Local Cheltenham Guide, * * * Illustrated with * * * an Itinerary of the Principal Roads; & a Table, shewing at one View, the relative Distances, by the great Roads, of all the Places of Public Resort from Cheltenham, & from each other, containing Nine Hundred Distances. *Second edition.* Bath, [1807?]. 12°.

The first edition of this Guide [Bath, 1803? 12°] has no Itinerary.

Mogg, Edward. A Survey of the Roads from London to Brighton, Southampton, Portsmouth, Hastings, Tunbridge Wells, Margate & Dover, laid down on a Scale of one Inch to a Mile. London, 1808. 4°.

Nicholson, George. The Cambrian Traveller's Guide, & Pocket Companion. Stourport, 1808. 8°.

— *Second edition*, corrected and considerably enlarged. Stourport, 1813. 8°.

— *Third edition*, revised and corrected by the Rev. Emilius Nicholson. London, 1840. 8°.

Attree, H. R. Attree's Topography of Brighton: &, Picture of the Roads, from thence to the Metropolis. 2 part. Brighton, 1809. 12°.

— *Second edition.* 2 part. Brighton, 1810. 12°.

Warner, Richard. A Tour through Cornwall in the autumn of 1808. By the Rev^d. Richard Warner, of Bath. Bath, 1809. 8°.

Cheltenham. The New & Improved Cheltenham Guide. Bath, [1810 *c*.]. 12°.

— *Second edition.* Bath, [1812 *c*.]. 12°.

— *A new edition.* Bath, [1816?]. 12°.

— The Cheltenham Guide. Cheltenham. 1811. 8°.
This may be an edition of the preceding Guide.

— The Improved Cheltenham Guide. Bath, [1815]. 12°.
Appears to be another issue of "The New & Improved Cheltenham Guide." *A new edition*; but, on wrapper: "*A Second Edition.*"

Perth. A Guide to the City of Perth & its Environs; & to the Principal Tours through the County. Perth, 1812. 8°.

— *Second edition.* Perth, 1813. 8°.

— Guide to the City & County of Perth. A Description of the Environs, & of the Principal Scenery in the County, in the form of Tours. *Fourth edition*, enlarged and embellished with maps, etc. Perth, 1822. 8°.

— *Another issue.* Perth, 1851. 8°.

Todd. Todd's Book of the Principal Post Roads in Great Britain, in which the Cities, Market-Towns, Villages, & Remarkable Places are inserted at their exact distance from each other. With a List of the Gentlemen's Seats, Etc. as they occur on the Road: Also Tables of the Expences of Posting. From Actual Surveys. London, 1812. 24°.

Cumberland. A Companion by the Way; or, a Guide to the Lakes, in Cumberland, Westmorland & Lancashire. From a late Survey. Penrith, 1812. 24°.

— *Third edition,* with additions. Penrith, 1826. 24°.
As "The Tourist's Guide to the Lakes, in Cumberland, Westmorland, & Lancashire."

Whittle, James, and Laurie, Richard Holmes. The Traveller's Guide to Paris: exhibiting the Roads from London, Havre, Dieppe, Boulogne, Calais, Dunkirk, Ostende, Ghent, & Antwerp, to Paris. Accurately laid down from the latest French Maps; with the postings, according to regulations made by the commissioners of the posts; descriptive remarks on the towns & villages on each road; & requisite extracts from the post regulations. London, 1814. 8°.

Mogg, Edward. A Survey of the High Roads of England & Wales & Part of Scotland planned on a Scale of 1 inch to a Mile. Nos. 1 to 10. London, 1814– . 4°.

Sickelmore, Richard, sen. An Epitome of Brighton, Topographical & Descriptive. Brighton, 1815. 12°.

— The History of Brighton; from the earliest period to the present time; & Picture of the Roads, by the three principal Routes, to the Metropolis. Brighton, 1823. 12°.

— Sickelmore's History of Brighton, & Picture of the Roads by the three principal Routes to the Metropolis. *Third edition.* Brighton, 1824. 12°.

Brighton. The Three Grand Routes from Brighton to London. Brighton, 1815. 12°.

With a "Picture of the Roads" separately paged.

Griffith, J. K. A General Cheltenham Guide, upon an entirely new plan. Cheltenham, [1815]. 12°.

— [*Second edition.*] Cheltenham, [1818]. 12°.

— *Another, second and new edition.* Cheltenham, [1819 c.]. 12°.

Scarborough. The Scarborough Guide. Scarborough, 1815. 12°.

— [*Fourth edition.*] Scarborough, 1821. 12°.

— *Another edition.* Scarborough, 1827. 12°.

Scotland. The Itinerary of Scotland; containing all the Direct & Cross Roads necessary for the information of the Traveller, & notice of every object which may contribute to his amusement. Edinburgh, 1816. 24°.

Edinburgh. The New Picture of Edinburgh for 1816, ＊ ＊ ＊ To which are added, a Description of Leith, & the Trosachs. Edinburgh, [1816]. 12°.

Mogg, Edward. Survey of the High Roads of England & Wales. Part the First. Comprising the Counties of Kent, Surrey, Sussex, Hants, Wilts, Dorset, Somerset, Devon & Cornwall; with Part of Buckingham & Middlesex. ＊ ＊ ＊ Arranged by & under the direction of Edward Mogg. London, 1817. 4°.

The plates are dated variously in 1814 and 1815. This appears to be a section of "A Survey of the High Roads of England & Wales & Part of Scotland" noted under the date 1814.

Europe. Atlas Portatif et Itinéraire de l'Europe, pour servir d'intelligence au guide de Voyageurs dans cette partie du Monde; composé de treize Cartes et Vues. A Paris, Chez Hyacinthe Langlois. Eighth edition. Paris, 1817. 8°.

Contains a *Carte routière d'Angleterre et de la partie méridionale de l'Ecosse.*

Wright, Charles. Rambles in the Vicinity of Brighton, to Lewes, Eastbourne, Worthing, Bramber, Devil's Dyke, Arundel, Etc. With an Itinerary of the Roads. Brighton, 1818. 12°.

— *Second edition,* improved, with a map of Sussex. Brighton, [1818]. 12°.

Brighton. A Journey to Brighton, through Stockwell, Clapham, Upper & Lower Tooting, Mitcham, Sutton, Gatton, Ryegate, Crawley, Cuckfield, Preston. Together with Brief Historical & Topographical Delineations of the above Towns, Villages, Gentlemen's Seats, Etc. With an Itinerary of the Road. London, 1818. 12°.

On the last page an "Itinerary of the Direct Road to Brighton, measured from the Surrey Side of Westminster Bridge."

Brighton. Excursion from London to Brighton, through Streatham, Croydon, Ryegate, Crawley, Cuckfield, & the New Road through Hicksted; containing Brief Historical & Topographical Delineations, Towns, Villages, Gentlemen's Seats, Etc. Forming a Complete Picture of the Road. London, 1818. 12°.

Appears to be a companion volume to the preceding.

Robinson, John. A Guide to the Lakes, in Cumberland, Westmorland, & Lancashire, illustrated with twenty views of Local Scenery, & a travelling map of the adjacent country. London, 1819. 8°.

Includes an "Itinerary from London to Penrith, in Cumberland; & from Kendal to London," and "Distances of Places in the Tour of the Lakes."

Lewis, William. Lewis's New Traveller's Guide, or a Pocket Edition of the English Counties, Containing all the Direct & Cross Roads in England & Wales. With the Distance of each Principal place from London. London, [1819]. 12°.

— *Another issue.* London, 1836. 12°.

Gandini, Francesco. Itinerario d'Europa di Francesco Gandini accuratamente riveduto corretto e considerabilmente aumentato dietro la guida dei viaggiatori in Europa del Sig. Reichard consigliere di guerra di S. A. il Duca di Sassonia-Gota. Second edition. Milan, 1819. 12°.

The British roads fill thirteen pages.

— *Itinéraire de l'Europe par François Gandini soigneusement revu, corrigé, et considérablement augmenté sur la guide des Voyageurs en Europe de M. Reichard conseiller de Guerre de S. A. le duc de Saxe-Gotha. Avec les derniers Règlemens authentiques des Administrations des Postes d'Italie, de France et d'Autriche. Fourth edition.* Milan, 1821. 8°.

A French version of the above.

Scotland. The Steam Boat Companion; & Stranger's Guide to the Western Islands & Highlands of Scotland; Comprehending the Land Tour of Inveraray & Oban. Glasgow, 1820. Tall 12°.

Second edition, greatly enlarged and improved. Glasgow, 1825. Tall 12°.

— Lumsden & Son's Steam-boat Companion; or Stranger's Guide to the Western Isles & Highlands of Scotland. *Third edition.* Glasgow, 1831. Tall 12°.

— *Another edition.* Glasgow, 1839. Tall 12°.

Cheltenham. The New Guide to Cheltenham: being a complete History & Description of that celebrated Watering Place. Cheltenham, [1820?]. 12°.

— *Another edition.* Cheltenham, [1822 c.]. 8°.

— *Another edition.* Cheltenham, 1823. 8°.

— William's New Guide to Cheltenham: being a complete History & Description of that celebrated Watering Place. Cheltenham, [1825]. 8°.

— A New Guide to Cheltenham. Cheltenham, [1825 c.]. 8°.

— *Another edition.* Cheltenham, 1829. 8°.

— *Another edition.* Cheltenham, 1830. 8°.

Gloucester. A New Guide to the City of Gloucester. ✱ ✱ ✱ With useful notices respecting the arrival & departure of the mail & other coaches. ✱ ✱ ✱ And several routes through the County. Gloucester, [1820 *c.*]. 12°.

— *Another edition.* Gloucester, [1822 *c.*]. 12°.

— *Another edition.* Gloucester, [1829 *c.*]. 12°.

Scotland. An Account of the Principal Pleasure Tours in Scotland; with a Copious Itinerary of the Great Lines of Roads, & the several Cross Roads in the Country. *Second edition*, with numerous corrections and additions. 2 part. Edinburgh, 1821. 8°.

— An Account of the Pleasure Tours in Scotland, illustrated by Maps, views of Remarkable Buildings, Etc. With an Itinerary. *Third edition.* 2 part. Edinburgh, 1824. 8°.

Paris. Tableaux Itinéraires des distances de Paris aux Principales Villes de France, et à toutes les Capitales d'Europe. Paris, 1821. 8°.

Sets out the roads from Paris to London, from London to Edinburgh, and from London to Dublin, as well as others in England.

England and Wales. An Account of the Principal Pleasure Tours of England & Wales. London, 1822. 8°.

Includes an "Itinerary of England," which gives the direct roads from London only.

Willett, Mark. The Stranger in Monmouthshire & South Wales; or, Illustrative Sketches of the History, Antiquities, & Scenery, of South Wales, & its Borders. With an Itinerary, Routes, Maps, & other Directions. Chepstow, [1822?]. 12°.

Otley, Jonathan. A Concise Description of the English Lakes, & adjacent Mountains: with General Directions to Tourists. Keswick, 1823. 8°.

— *Second edition.* Keswick, 1825. 8°.

— *Third edition.* Keswick, 1827. 8°.

— *Fourth edition.* Keswick, 1830. 8°.

— *Fifth edition.* Keswick, 1834. 8°.

— *Sixth edition.* Keswick, 1837. 8°.

— *Sixth edition.* Keswick, 1838. 8°.

Scotland. Principal Roads through Scotland, from Edinburgh, Glasgow, etc.; including the Usual Tours by the Forts along the Caledonian Canal, & to Loch Katrine; Great Roads to London * * * *Second edition,* improved. Edinburgh, 1823. 8°.

— *Another edition.* Edinburgh, 1827. 8°.

Gray, George Carrington. The Tourist & Traveller's Guide to the Roads of England & Wales, & part of Scotland, on an entirely new plan. London, 1824. 8°.

Prichard, Thomas Jeffery Llewelyn. The New Aberystwyth Guide to the Waters, Bathing Houses, Public Walks, & Amusements. Aberystwyth, 1824. 8°.

Leigh, Samuel. Leigh's New Pocket Road-Book of England & Wales, & Part of Scotland * * * containing an account of all the Direct & Cross Roads; together with a Description of every Remarkable Place, its Curiosities, Manufactures, Commerce, Population, & Principal Inns. London, 1825. 12°.

— *Another edition.* London, 1826. 12°.

— *Third edition.* London, 1831. 12°.

— *Fourth edition.* London, 1833. 12°.

— *Fifth edition.* London, 1835. 12°.

— *Sixth edition.* London, 1837. 12°.

— *Seventh edition.* London, 1839. 12°.

— *Eighth edition.* London, 1840. 12°.

There is also a French translation of this road book published by Richard, London, 1828–29. 12°.

Cambridge. The Stranger's Companion; forming a Complete Guide through the University & Town of Cambridge; * * * *Second edition.* Cambridge, 1825. 12°.

Scotland. The Scottish Tourist, & Itinerary; or, a Guide to the Scenery & Antiquities of Scotland & the Western Islands. Edinburgh, 1825. 8°.

— *Second edition*, with considerable additions and improvements. Edinburgh, 1827. 8°.

— *Fourth edition.* Edinburgh, 1832. 8°.

— *Fifth edition.* Edinburgh, 1834. 8°.

— *Sixth edition*, with very considerable additions and improvements. Edinburgh, 1836. 8°.

— *Eighth edition.* Edinburgh, 1842. 8°.

— The Scottish Tourist; being a Guide to the Picturesque Scenery & Antiquities of Scotland * * * in which the Geology & Botany are largely introduced. Illustrated with * * * Travelling Maps, & engraved Routes. *Ninth edition.* Edited by William Rhind. Edinburgh, 1845. 8°.

Bath. Collings's Improved Bath Guide. Bath, [1825]. 8°.

Chester. The Traveller's Companion in an Excursion from Chester through North Wales. Chester, [1825]. 16°.

Quétin, Louis. Nouvel Itinéraire portatif de la Grande-Bretagne, comprenant L'Angleterre, L'Ecosse, et L'Irlande. Paris, [1825?]. 12°.

— *Another edition.* London, 1828. 12°.

— *New edition.* Paris, 1836 [and 1837]. 12°.

One of the *Collection Européenne de Nouveaux Itinéraires Portatifs, à l'usage des Voyageurs.*

Smith, Charles. Smith's New Pocket Companion to the Roads of England & Wales & Part of Scotland. Engraved on Forty-three Copper Plates. Comprehending the Routes from London to every considerable Town in England & Wales, & the principal Cross Roads. London, 1826. 8°.

— *Another edition.* London, 1827. 8°.

— *Another edition.* London, 1830. 8°.

Mogg, Edward. Mogg's Pocket Itinerary of the Direct & Cross Roads of England & Wales, with part of the Roads of Scotland. London, 1826. 12°.

— *Another edition.* London, [1833]. 12°.

The preface of this edition is dated "May 18, 1833"*.

Griffith, Samuel Young. Griffith's New Historical Description of Cheltenham & its Vicinity. Cheltenham, 1826. 4°.

---

* In the title appears "To which is now first added, an Appendix of the Rail Roads." Bound in at the end, with a separate title and pagination, is an "Appendix to Mogg's Pocket Itinerary; being a Description of the Rail Roads, at present in operation for the conveyance of passengers in various parts of the Kingdom. By Edward Mogg, Editor of the New & Improved Edition of Paterson's Roads." London, 1837. 12°.

This publication is claimed, in the "Explanatory Remarks," as being the first appearance of Rail Roads in an itinerary, and it thus marks the commencement of a new period in the bibliography of road-books and itineraries. Nine Railways are described in road-book form, in twelve pages, namely: Birmingham to Liverpool by the Grand Junction Railway; Liverpool and Manchester Railway; Pickering and Whitby Railway; Leeds and Selby Railway; Bolton and Leigh and Kenyon Junction Railway; Newcastle and Carlisle Railway; Stockton and Darlington Railroad; The Greenwich Rail-Way, and London and Birmingham Railway ("at present travellable only to Boxmoor").

Griffith, Samuel Young. New Historical Description of Cheltenham & its Vicinity, dedicated to the King's most excellent Majesty. Cheltenham, 1826. 8°.

— *Second edition.* London, 1826. 8°.

— *Third edition.* Cheltenham, 1828. 8°.

Lake, W. Itinéraire Descriptif et Topographique des Routes de Paris à Londres. Paris, 1826. 18°.

Brighton. Brighton by the Five Great Roads. New & Improved Itinerary, of all the principal Roads in Great Britain, illustrative of each place of note, & comprising every information of interest to travellers. Published in separate Roads. Price 1*s.* 6*d.* London, 1827. 8°.

Mottershead, Jasper. The Traveller's Guide from London to Holyhead, & from London to Birmingham, Liverpool, Manchester, Edinburgh, ✳ ✳ ✳ to which is added an amusing collection of Travelling Anecdotes, with a Map of the Roads. Shrewsbury, 1827. 16°.

— The Traveller's Guide, or Topographical Remembrancer; describing the Route from London to Holyhead, by way of Coventry, Birmingham, Shrewsbury, Capel Curig, & Menai Bridge. The same, by way of Oxford: Journies from London to Liverpool, by way of Newcastle, & Warrington, from London to Edinburgh, by way of Manchester & Carlisle, with a description of intermediate Towns, Villages, Antiquities, Curiosities, etc. *Third edition.* Shrewsbury, [1831?]. 16°.

Harper. Harper's New Cheltenham Guide; containing a Copious Itinerary. Cheltenham, [1827 *c.*]. 12°.

Donne, Benjamin. The Traveller's Guide through England, Wales & part of Scotland, containing the distance measured from Bristol in the great & direct roads; likewise the distance measured from Town to Town. Bristol, 1829. 12°.

Leigh, Samuel. Leigh's New Pocket Road-Book of Scotland, containing an account of all the Direct & Cross Roads; together with a Description of every Remarkable Place, its Curiosities, Manufactures, Commerce, Population, & principal Inns. London, 1829. 12°.

— *New edition.* London, 1836. 12°.

— *Third edition.* London, 1839. 12°.

— *Another edition.* London, 1840. 12°.

Baines, Edward, jun. A Companion to the Lakes of Cumberland. Westmoreland, & Lancashire; with a new, copious & correct Itinerary, London, 1829. 12°.

— *Another edition.* London, 1834. 12°.

Leigh, Samuel. Leigh's Guide to the Lakes & Mountains of Cumberland, Westmoreland, & Lancashire. London, 1830. 12°.

— *Second edition.* London, 1832. 12°.

— *Third edition.* London, 1835. 12°.

— *Fourth edition.* London, 1840. 12°.

Cheltenham. The History of Cheltenham, & Visitor's Guide; * * * To which is added, a Copious Itinerary, of the Routes & Distances through the country, intended as "A Pocket Companion" for the Visitor & Resident. Cheltenham, [1830]. 12°.

England and Wales. A Correct Table of the Distances of the principal towns of England & Wales, from London; also shewing the Distances they are from each other. Together with a List of all the Market Towns, the days on which the Markets are held, & how far distant from London. London, [1830?]. Large sheet.

Leigh, Samuel. Leigh's Guide to Wales & Monmouthshire: containing observations on the mode of travelling, plans of various tours, etc. London, 1831. 12°.

— *Second edition.* London, 1833. 12°.

— *Fourth edition.* London, 1839. 12°.

— *Sixth edition.* London, 1841. 12°.

Bruce, John. The History of Brighton, with the latest improvements, to 1831. Brighton, [1831]. 12°.

— [*Second edition.*] Brighton, [1833]. 12°.

— *Third edition.* Brighton, [1834]. 12°.

— *Fourth edition,* Brighton, [1835]. 12°.

— *Fourth edition,* Brighton, [1837]. 12°.

Contains a table of distances from Brighton, and the London and cross country routes from that town.

Buzonnière, Léon de. Voyage en Ecosse, ou Itinéraire Général de l'Ecosse. Paris, 1832. 8°.

Devonport. The Topographer; or Pedestrian's Companion to the principal Bye-ways within nine miles of Devonport & Plymouth, & most of the favourite walks of the late N. T. Carrington. Devonport, 1833. 12°.

Anderson, George, and Anderson, Peter. Guide to the Highlands & Islands of Scotland, including Orkney & Zetland, descriptive of their scenery, statistics, antiquities, & natural history: with numerous historical notes. London, 1834. 8°.

— — *New edition.* Edinburgh, 1842. 8°.

— — *Third edition,* carefully revised, enlarged and remodelled. Edinburgh, 1850. 8°.

— — *Third edition*, carefully revised, enlarged and remodelled. Edinburgh, 1851. 8°.

Phippen, James. The Road Guide from London to Tunbridge Wells: through Lewisham, Bromley, Farnborough, Sevenoaks, Tunbridge. London, 1836. 12°.

Olivieri, Charles L[ro]. *Tableau de toutes les Routes de Poste de l'Europe.* London, 1836. Large sheet.

Includes "20 *Routes partant de Londres pour l'Angleterre, l'Ecosse et l'Irlande.*"

Brady, John Henry. The Dover Road Sketch Book; or, Traveller's Pocket Guide, between London & Dover, wherein is described every object of interest on this Road. Canterbury, 1837. 8°.

Anderson, John, jun. Anderson's Tourist's Guide through Scotland, upon a new & improved plan; with maps & charts illustrative of the Principal Pleasure Tours. Edinburgh, 1837. 16°.

Contains "An Itinerary of the leading Post-Roads throughout the Country."

Davidson, G. H. The Thames & Thanet Guide, & Kentish Tourist: containing the History & Description, Topographical, Antiquarian, Statistical, & Legendary, of Every Place & Object of Note between London Bridge & Ramsgate Harbour; A Road Book from London to Dover, Margate, Ramsgate, Sandwich, Deal, Etc. *Third edition.* London, [1838]. 12°.

— *Fifth edition.* London, [1840]. 12°.

— *Sixth edition.* London, no date. 12°.

Scotland. The Scottish Land Tourist's Pocket Guide. To which is now added, an appendix containing the principal Roads through Scotland. Glasgow, 1839. 16°.

— *Another edition.* Glasgow, 1850. 16°.

Harvey, John. Alphabetical List of the Cities & Towns in England & Wales, with their County, Distance, & number of Stages from Weymouth. Weymouth, 1839. 8°.

Onwhyn, Joseph. Onwhyn's Guide to the Highlands of Scotland; or, The Pedestrian's Pocket Companion. London, 1839. 24°.

— *Another edition.* London, 1841. 24°.

Onwhyn, Joseph. Onwhyn's Welsh Tourist; or, New Guide to North & South Wales, & the Wye: * * * Illustrated with a Map of Route. London, 1840. 12°.

Black, Adam and Charles. Black's Picturesque Tourist of Scotland. With an accurate Travelling Map; * * * & a copious Itinerary. Edinburgh, 1840. 12°.

— *Second edition.* Edinburgh, [1840]. 12°.

— *Second edition.* Edinburgh, 1842. 12°.

— *Third edition.* Edinburgh, 1843. 12°.

— *Third edition.* Edinburgh, 1844. 12°.

— *Fourth edition.* Edinburgh, 1845. 12°.

And numerous subsequent editions.

England. The Journey-Book of England.

Berkshire. London, 1840. 4°.

Derbyshire. London, 1841. 4°.

Hampshire; including the Isle of Wight. London, 1841. 4°.

Kent. London, 1842. 4°.

Issued in parts, of which only the above were printed. Each part contains a short section on means of communication and traffic, with some account of the roads and a table of distances.

Poppele, E. Manuel des Postes pour l'Allemagne et les routes principales de l'Europe. Avec des notices très-avantageuses pour ceux qui prennent la poste, les voitures accélérées, les bateaux à vapeur, les chemins de fer; reductions des monnaies etc. Accompagné d'une carte routière et d'une table de plus de 2500 routes de voyage. Cinquième édition, complètement revue, augmentée et améliorée. Frankfort, 1840. 8°.

Out of five hundred routes four relate to the British Isles, namely: Frankfort to Dublin; Frankfort to Edinburgh; Frankfort to London, (i) by Calais, (ii) by Ostend, and (iii) by Helvütslys; and Frankfort to Manchester. There is a German version also of this guide. Frankfort, 1840. 8°.

Phippen, James. Colbran's New Guide for Tunbridge Wells, being a full & accurate Description of the Wells & its neighbourhood, within a circuit of nearly twenty miles. Tunbridge Wells, 1840. 12°.

— *Second edition.* Tunbridge Wells, [1846?]. 12°.
And later issues.

Phippen, James. Colbran's New Guide for Tunbridge Wells, (abridged,) being an Accurate Description of the Wells & its neighbourhood, within a circuit of nearly twenty miles. Tunbridge Wells, 1840. 12°.

— *Another edition.* Tunbridge Wells, 1844. 12°.

Davies, Henry. The Visitor's Hand-Book for Cheltenham. Cheltenham, 1840. 12°.
Includes an "Itinerary to some of the Principal Places in England & Wales."

Black, Adam and Charles. Black's Picturesque Guide to the English Lakes, with a copious Itinerary. Edinburgh, 1841. 12°.

— *Second edition.* Edinburgh, 1845. 12°.
— *Fifth edition.* Edinburgh, 1851. 12°.
And many subsequent editions.

Onwhyn, Joseph. Onwhyn's Pocket Guide to the Lakes; or, tourist's companion to the beauties of Cumberland, Westmoreland, & Lancashire. London, 1841. 12°.

Sussex. The Miniature Road-Book of Sussex. Shewing the distances & routes from one town to another, & from each to London, on an entirely new plan. With a Map, a Population Table comprising the census of 1841, & various other topographical information. London, [1841?]. 32°.

In the preface it is stated that "The whole of the Counties of England, treated in the same manner, will form four small volumes," but the following of these road-books only are known to have been subsequently issued.

Hampshire. The Miniature Road-Book of Hampshire. London, [1842]. 32°.

Isle of Wight. The Miniature Road-Book of the Isle of Wight. London, [1842]. 32°.

Kent. The Miniature Road-Book of Kent. London, [1842]. 32°.

Surrey. The Miniature Road-Book of Surrey. London, [1842]. 32°.

England. Reciprocal Distances of the principal towns of England, Ireland, Scotland, & Wales; with some of the principal travelling stations of France & the Netherlands, from each other & from London. Leeds, 1842. Single sheet.

This is a large sheet of tables, with itineraries of coach routes, of mail coach routes, and of railways, and many other particulars.

Black, Adam and Charles. Black's Picturesque Tourist & Road-Book of England & Wales. Edinburgh, 1843. 12°.

— Black's Picturesque Tourist & Road & Railway Guide Book through England & Wales. *Second edition*, greatly enlarged and improved. Edinburgh, 1851. 12°.

Followed by many subsequent editions.

Parry, Edward. The Cambrian Mirror, or North Wales Tourist. Chester, 1843. 16°.

— Cambrian Mirror; or, a new Tourist Companion through North Wales. *Second edition.* London, 1846. 16°.

— *Another issue*, as the "*Second Edition.*" London, 1847. 16°.

— The Cambrian Mirror; or, The Tourist's Companion through North Wales. *Another issue.*—Eighth Thousand. London, 1851. 16°.

Hudson, John. A Complete Guide to the Lakes, comprising Minute Directions for the Tourist. *Second edition.* Kendal, 1843. 12°.

— *Fourth edition.* Kendal, 1853. 12°.

— *Fifth edition.* London, 1859. 12°.

Hastings. The Hand-Book for Hastings, St Leonard's & their neighbourhood. Hastings, 1845. 8°.

Ross, Thomas. Ross's Hastings & St Leonard's Guide, containing a variety of information respecting the History & Antiquities of the above & Neighbouring Towns, with a full description of all subjects necessary to the Comfort & Accommodation of Visitors. Hastings, [1845]. 16°.

"The Distances of Roads from Hastings to London; & the Coast Road from Margate to Portsmouth" are included.

— *Second edition.* Hastings, 1851. 12°.

Devonshire. The Route Book of Devon. Exeter, [1845]. 12°.

— *Second edition.* Exeter, [1846]. 12°.

And editions of [1871] and [1877].

Hicklin, John. Excursions in North Wales: a complete Guide to the Tourist through that Romantic Country; containing descriptions of its Picturesque Beauties, Historical Antiquities & Modern Wonders. London, 1847. 16°.

— *Fifth thousand.* London, 1851. 16°.

Cumberland. A Complete & Descriptive Guide to the Lakes of Cumberland, Westmorland, & Lancashire. Ulverston, 1847. 12°.

North Wales. The Cambrian Tourist Guide & Companion, containing a concise Account & Description of North Wales: chiefly in the Counties of Merioneth & Caernarvon. Dolgelley, 1847. 12°.

Great Britain and Ireland. Nouveau Guide du Voyageur en Angleterre, en Ecosse, et en Irlande, suivi d'un voyage d'agrément aux endroits les plus pittoresques de chaque contrée, * * * *d'après Leigh's new pocket road-book of England* * * * *par Richard.* * * * *Ouvrage entièrement neuf, orné d'une excellente carte routière.* London, 1849. 18°.

Smith, William. The Particular Description of England. With the Portratures of Certaine of the Cheiffest Citties & Townes. 1588. With views of some of the chief towns & armorial bearings of Nobles & Bishops. Edited, from the original MS. in the British Museum, with an introduction by Henry B. Wheatley & Edmund W. Ashbee. London, 1879. 4°.

"The High Wais, from any notable towne in England to the Cittie of London, & Lykewyse from one notable towne to another" include twelve roads and twenty-nine cross-roads and variations of routes.

INDEX

OF NAMES OF AUTHORS, PUBLISHERS AND PRINTERS